CHASING
MY DREAM

CHASING MY DREAM

JOURNEY INTO
THE WORLD OF WRITING

WEI LIEM NG

PARTRIDGE
A Penguin Random House Company

To order additional copies of this book, contact
Toll Free 800 101 2657 (Singapore)
Toll Free 1 800 81 7340 (Malaysia)
orders.singapore@partridgepublishing.com

www.partridgepublishing.com/singapore

Contents

Thank you from the bottom of my heart to Mom, Dad, and Bro for your words of encouragement.
I love you guys very much.
Special thanks to my friends Rui Ming, Suet Ping, Tong Seng, Tat Liang, Berenice, Wee Vian, Vin Shern, Pei San, Yong Hui, Koh Sin, and Colin for being in my life.
Huge thanks to those who read my book.
I am forever grateful for your support.
I hope that happiness will always be around you.

Dear Readers

HI THERE. MY ACTUAL NAME is Wei Liem Ng, but people just call me William. Trust me: it is easier to pronounce it that way. Anyway, I will cut to the chase.

If you are looking for a self-improvement book to tell you the steps you should take to chase your dreams, this book is not right for you. You can put it down now.

This book is more than that. It is a collection of my experiences as an accountant from my first day of working at a construction company until my very last. It contains my thoughts, my feelings, and every memorable encounter that I went through. I would like to sit down with you and tell you all about my journey over a cup of coffee, but I would be too nervous to say anything. So, I have decided to invite you into my world by writing a book about my funny, sad, happy, and overall great journey from accountant to writer. You see, I've always dreamt about becoming a writer. Therefore, I name this book "Chasing My Dream". I use the word "my" for a reason: it is about me chasing *my* dream. Ultimately, every person has a different dream.

I apologize in advance if sixty per cent of my book sounds depressing. What can I say? Becoming an accountant is depressing, after all. It is easier to blame the job than own up to my problems. To be honest, it is me who is dark and gloomy all the time. I am constantly overwhelmed by my negative perception.

But if you are still reading this, I sincerely thank you for your support. By the end of this book, I hope that you will be a different person, a person who has the courage to chase your own dreams like I did. If you are already living your dream, I hope that you have a great laugh at my experience and think, "I am so glad that my life is better than his!" I wish you all the best in your future. Deep within my heart, I hope that in some wacky or good way, this book can inspire you to live your life to the fullest. After all, YOLO (You Only Live Once), right?

Good luck and happy reading.

With much gratitude,
Wei Liem Ng

First of all

Daydreaming at Night

MY HOUSE IS SITUATED IN the middle of nowhere, surrounded by lush green trees. I guess this is why people call that area the Green Acre Residence. Very often, I wondered why my parents settled here. Why are my neighbours here? There is nothing exciting to do here except watch trees grow. Have you ever stared at a tree and watched it grow? Trust me: it gets boring after a while.

Every night is the same in my house. At exactly eleven o'clock, every one of my family members is already sound asleep. The whole house is quiet, so quiet that the ticking sound made by the clock on the wall becomes clear in my ears. I would walk into my room to escape the ticking noise. My room is my safe haven; I've always like a small, quiet space all to myself. I can hear my footsteps when I walk. I can hear every breath I take. And, most importantly, I can hear myself think.

My hobby is daydreaming. My mind often wanders off on its own into the land of imagination. Sadly, daydreaming gets a bad reputation. The majority of the people I know reject my hobby. Since I was young, I have been told that daydreaming is bad, daydreaming is stupid, and daydreaming is a waste of time. But I believe that daydreaming gives my life unlimited opportunities. It helps me to see the world not as it is but as it can be. It gives me hope about the uncertain future I am about to explore, filling my days with fun and adventure. Someday, I want to tell myself, "You did it. You made your dream come true."

I often share my dream with my close friends, Yap and Ping. The more I share my dream, the more I realize that daydreaming is not a waste of time; it is a wonderful gift, and it belongs to every great man and woman. Those who are successful have it. Those who are more successful dare to chase their dreams. This is what life is all about, right? Having a dream and chasing it with all your heart.

Walt Disney once said, "It all started with a mouse". I am sure he was a person who daydreamt a lot, spending most of his time doodling on papers about a mouse that talked and sang. Eventually, he made his dream a reality by becoming the most well-known cartoonist and animator who ever walked this earth. That was a shining example of the fact that daydreaming *is* a positive hobby.

I have always dreamt about writing my own book, but I could never find the courage to publish it. So, my dream became a series of Word documents with fancy titles arranged neatly in a folder, idling on my computer desktop.

The "Yin" and "Yang" of My Life

WITH THE HELP OF SOCIAL media, people willingly partake in popularity contests. The more friends you have, the more socially acceptable you are. Having friends on social media shows how likable you are, never mind if they barely talk to you in real life or even share your interests. All of those are not important. As long as your Facebook page is flooded with birthday comments that are probably copied and pasted from other websites, which you probably won't even bother to read, it doesn't matter. It is good enough; it means that they are your friends. It means that they care enough to post a comment on your page, although most of them are probably reminded by the Facebook admin about your birthday.

Quantity of friends seems to be the craze these days. As for me, it is never about the quantity of friends I have. It is the quality of friends I have that makes my life wonderful.

I have two close friends. OK, technically I only have two friends. They are Yap and Ping. I categorize the rest as my acquaintances who listen to my rants from time to time.

Yap and Ping are complete opposites. They are as different as night and day, which is why I call them the "Yin" and "Yang" of my life.

First of all, Yap is a male and Ping is a female. Yap is a man of science. He studied the science stream in secondary school and dedicated his life to becoming a dentist. Meanwhile, Ping is a woman of art. She studied the art stream in secondary school and dedicated her life to becoming an artist. Yap sees the world as mathematics equation. Everyone plays a part as a number to complete the equation, advancing society into a scientific future. Ping sees the world as a white canvas. Everyone serves as her paint: some colour her life, some dull her life, and all of them come together to help create her masterpiece.

For as long as I can remember, my friendship with Yap is built upon the foundation of liking the same things. We appreciate good books and use words of encouragement to motivate each other. He sees the silver lining in every tragic ordeal. He tells me that whatever I want to do in my life, I must make sure that it brings hope to society, just as Dalai Lama once said, "It is necessary to help others, not only in our prayers, but in our daily lives". He consistently reminds me that if I am successful one day, I should help every unfortunate soul and make the world a better place.

On the contrary, my friendship with Ping is built upon the foundation of hating the same things, such as the boring nine-to-five working hours. Our main mode of communication is using sarcasm to assault each other to see who gets pissed off first. She sees mostly negativity in everything and encourages me to eat a lot of meat because "we didn't climb all the way to the top of the food chain just to eat grass". She believes that no one is obliged to be nice to one another – "just because you are a vegetarian, doesn't mean that the lion won't eat you when it is hungry". She warns me not to care about anyone's opinion and do what I love most.

Two of them have strong personal opinions that contradict one another. But even so, every time I need help, they come to my aid, be it by using positive words to encourage me or offensive words to sass me until I realize my mistakes. I spent countless years trying to figure out the reason I befriended them in the first place.

Today the answer is clear to me. Despite their differences, they have one thing in common: they have big dreams, and they aren't afraid to pursue their dreams.

The Exam from Hell

THROUGHOUT COLLEGE, I STUDIED DILIGENTLY for my accounting degree, passing every exam with flying colours. I was on cloud nine. I thought that I could conquer the business world! Everything went well for me, until I took the ACCA (Association of Chartered Certified Accountants) exams.

They were like hell for me. The exams were designed to kill my brain cells by making me analyze complicated case studies accompanied by complex figures. As if the case studies weren't confusing enough, the exams promoted mental diarrhea by making my brain discharge numerous accounting standards that I normally didn't even bother to remember. To top it all off, all those painstaking questions needed to be answered within three hours, and I had to score fifty marks to pass the exams.

I took my final paper during December, and my results would be released on 8 February 2013 at exactly 2:00 p.m., which also happened to be two days before Chinese New Year. That left me with two possible outcomes: either I was going to have a happy Chinese New Year or a crappy Chinese New Year.

It was already two twenty in the afternoon, and yet there was still no message from the ACCA exam board members. Each time my phone made a beep, I had a miniature heart attack.

It is exactly like the feeling when I text my crush and hold my phone next to me, hoping helplessly for the moment she replies me. The anxiety is so great that it consumes me, and I am rendered incapable of doing anything except wait for her text message. Each time my phone makes its familiar beep, I can't help but quickly check for a sign that my crush acknowledges me and replies to my message. More often than not, it is not her message, and I feel that all hope is lost. When my phone beeps again, suddenly my spirit is lifted; hope has been restored again. The vicious cycle repeats endlessly until I get her text message, the one that I have been waiting for all day, the one that matters the most. Only then will I be relieved from my anxiety. A few minutes later, I will text another message to her, sending the whole vicious cycle into motion once more. Stupid, right?

All I wanted that day was to pass my exams. I wanted to have a wonderful Chinese New Year. I deserved a wonderful Chinese New Year, considering the amount of effort I had put into my studies. I was already daydreaming about my wonderful Chinese New Year, full of cheer and laughter. There was going to be good food, firecrackers, and relatives celebrating my achievement.

Suddenly, my phone made the familiar beeping sound, snapping me out of my trance. I browsed frantically for that important message. Finally, I had received my results. As my eyes scanned through the message again and again, I realized that that was it. That was my moment of truth.

I had passed my ACCA exams! I had achieved what every accountant dreamt of. I got my professional certification. Nothing could get in my way. All the sweat, tears, and blood had been worth it. I had sacrificed so much, and I had passed my final paper. Sure, I had just cleared the passing threshold of fifty marks, but still, I passed. It was a great day for me.

I let out a sigh of relief as I browsed my Facebook page to spy on my course mates. I needed to know their results, but I wasn't the kind of person who knew how to celebrate other people's victories, and I also didn't know how to console them about their failures either. Thus, spying on them through Facebook was my best option.

For those who passed the exams, some engaged in the textbook-burning ritual, a ritual that signifies "screw this! I am so done with ACCA exams!" Others who were more well-to-do planned their trips across the globe to ensure that they would have a fun-filled adventure before starting the next chapter of their lives.

For those who failed the exams, some decided to shut the world out and wallowed in self-pity while thinking about the unbearable experience of having to go through hell once more. Others resorted to alcohol therapy, a method deemed to be effective in temporarily drowning away their sorrow.

As for me, I did nothing the entire day except lay in my bed watching *Friends*, my favourite TV series. It was rather ironic, since I didn't have friends to hang out with, mainly because I had committed social suicide by burying my head in revision notes and textbooks for the past few months.

A Place Called
Kuala Terengganu

WRITING MY RESUME PROVED TO be a challenge. I was surprised that filling up my resume could easily cost me three days and yet writing about my life experiences in my journal took less than three hours. It was the same thing. I was just writing about myself.

After the excruciatingly boring process of writing my resume, I made a new discovery about myself. It was obvious that I wasn't cut out to be a formal person. I wrote stories, not facts in bullet format. I could already foresee a miserable future as an accountant.

"What have I got myself into? Why did I choose to become an accountant and not a writer? Oh wait! This is Malaysia we are talking about. The country doesn't exactly support young writers," I told myself constantly. So, I had to choose one of the most secure jobs in the world, accounting.

Among the two-page statement about all my past achievements, there was one segment that I enjoyed writing. It was about the interesting internship experience I had during my final year in college.

During my internship with an international company, I was placed under the supervision of a very inquisitive boss. As a foreigner, he was ever so fascinated with the place I came from, Kuala Terengganu. Every day at 6:30 p.m., he would summon me into his room for his so-called "brainstorming" session. And by brainstorming, I meant that he Googled interesting things about Kuala Terengganu and piled his questions one by one onto me until I filled his curiosity with satisfactory answers – supported by evidence, of course. I was generally happy to share my experiences growing up in Kuala Terengganu. Often, I would give him detailed descriptions of our culture, together with the pictures I searched on Google, just like he did. Sometimes, when I got a little tired of his never-ending questions, I started to make up stories and intertwine them with some facts just to mess with him.

Terengganu is one of the thirteen states in Malaysia. The capital of Terengganu is Kuala Terengganu. If you translate that name directly, it means "Terengganu confluence". A confluence is the junction of two rivers, especially rivers of approximately equal width. I just learnt that by using Google's dictionary. The locals call Kuala Terengganu "KT". There are several islands surrounding Terengganu, and the best-known ones are Pulau Kapas (Cotton Island), Pulau Redang (Redand Island), and Pulau Lang Tengah (Middle Lang Island). Please note that I translate the words directly, so the name doesn't make any sense.

Although KT is the capital of the state, it is more like a small town, surrounded by beautiful green trees and sapphire blue sea. The people in KT live in trees, and our main mode of transport is walking across wooden bridges to reach another tree house. We choose to live in our tree houses because there are many dangerous animals lurking on the ground. For the places where we can't build our wooden bridge, we swing from vines to vines in order to arrive at our destination. To go to work or school, we ride animals such as elephants, rhinos and horses, whichever that pass by our tree house first. As for those who live on the islands, their main mode of transport is riding turtles. After centuries of living with animals, we have developed a mutual communication method with the animals. Here in KT, humans and animals live happily together.

Just so you know, the paragraph above is pure nonsense. I made that up just to confuse my supervisor and to spark his curiosity so that one day he may visit my hometown. I wanted him to see with his own eyes that the people in Kuala Terengganu aren't aborigines who hunt animals for a living. We are civilized people just like him! If he decided to visit me in Kuala Terengganu, there would be plenty of places for him to tour around.

Living in a small town all my life, I wanted to go to the big city for a change. According to rumours, opportunities were everywhere, and I just had to be brave enough to get them. Without hesitation, I applied for a job in Kuala Lumpur, or as the locals call it, KL, which means "muddy confluence". Seriously, I am not one to complain, but Malaysia needs to come up with nicer names for its places.

An Awkward Interview

MY FIRST INTERVIEW EXPERIENCE WAS awkward. I remember sitting on a black leather couch that was so big, I felt like I was being swallowed by it. My feet couldn't touch the ground as I sank deeper and deeper into the leather. It was soft enough to push my ears against the side of my head, shutting out the typing noise made by the secretary as her acrylic nails hit the keyboard. Suddenly, I noticed the piercing gaze from her eyes, and I returned her gaze with a smile. She immediately rolled her eyes and fixed her sight onto the computer screen again. I pushed my feet to reach the ground and sat up straight like a meerkat sensing danger. I should sit up straight, with no slouching. I was in an interview, and first impressions were extremely important.

As an accountant, my choices were limited. At least, I thought they were limited. There were three options: to work in accounting firms, banking firms, or commercial firms. I didn't want to work in an accounting firm. The thought of becoming an auditor and working in an accounting firm haunted me. My university lecturer once made a joke about auditors. She told me that sometimes they would be treated as guard dogs to prevent money laundering and fraud. Other times, they would be treated as bloodhounds, sniffing out any attempt to breach corporate conduct. Most of the time, they were just monkeys because they were paid peanuts.

Banking firms were a big no-no to me as well. Rumours had it that as an accountant in a bank, I would be staring at money coming in and money going out on a daily basis. Life would be so monotonous that I would be better off becoming a robot.

That left me with only one option, to embark on my career in a commercial firm. Of all the commercial firms, I chose a construction company. I figured that if I could witness a house being built from scratch, it wouldn't be as boring as staring at the computer all day.

"William, right? Are you ready?" The voice of the secretary interrupted my thoughts. Before I could open my mouth, she said, "The HR personnel will see you now." As I walked past her to go into the interview room, I smiled at her again, hoping for a reply, but she focused intensely on her computer screen and continued typing, just like an emotionless robot. Maybe she should work in a bank.

The interview lasted for two hours, longer than what I had pictured. Aside from the mentally challenging tests that I needed to complete within a certain time frame, the interview questions were downright difficult. Every time I answered a question, the interviewer frantically jotted something on her notepad. Her eyes were fixed on her paper. I could see her eyeballs shifting from left to right as she wrote, not bothering to make eye contact with me. It was a horrible experience. I felt like I was talking to a wall shaped like a person.

Questions and Answers

BEFORE ATTENDING MY INTERVIEW, I did my homework. I Googled "top three questions that interviewers ask", knowing that my answers to those questions would strengthen my credibility as a job applicant.

Question number one was "Why should we hire you?" or "What makes you the best candidate for this job?"

Every company wants to hire a hard worker, but it is hard to gauge whether a person is hardworking or not during an interview, so you have to tell the interviewer how hardworking you are. Also, always remember to include what you can contribute to the company and what the company can do for you.

I answered, "I am a dedicated and hardworking person, as proven by my university results, and I will be a great addition to the team as an accountant. I have always wanted to work in the construction industry because I love observing the transformation of a barren land into a fully functional building."

In my heart, I couldn't believe I said that. That was so not how I would've answered the question. If I were speaking honestly, I would've said something like, "Why should you hire me? Because I am way more creative and lively compared to most of the people here, especially that zombie secretary with the long nails. And yes, I am a great addition to the team, because the company looks dead from the outside and it is dead on the inside as well. I can definitely spark things up with my creativity!"

Question number two was "Where do you see yourself three/five/seven years from now?"

The number of years doesn't matter. The point of the question is to understand your medium- to long-term goals. You should answer as though you were already a manager at the company and not make tacky promises, like you are going to stay loyal to the company because it is your dream job. Interviewers can sense a lie when they hear one.

I answered, "I see myself sharing my accounting knowledge with my team members as well as taking on new challenges. If I have the chance to lead a team, I hope that my team can contribute efficiently and effectively towards the company."

I fought hard to hold in my laughter. A real answer would've been, "Are you kidding me? Obviously, I see myself in a mirror. To be 100 per cent honest, in five years, I hope that I no longer have to work for money and buying luxury goods is not an issue for me. I don't have to be a billionaire – a millionaire will do. Please pay me a high salary so that I can achieve my goal. Who am I kidding? That will *never* happen."

Question number three was "Why do you want to work in this company?"

The question is not to be used to praise yourself by saying that you are a valuable asset and you can job hop to any company. It is a dare. Or it is more like a test to see whether you are suitable for the company. The correct answer is always to describe how well the company had done in the past and how proud you will be to work for such a great company.

I answered, "This company is one of the most outstanding construction companies in Malaysia. I am certain that it can provide me the opportunities that I need, and considering the diversity of the projects it undertakes, I want to have a great portfolio of experiences working as an accountant in this company."

Actually, I struggled with that question, mainly because I wanted to be a writer. I didn't know why I was there for the interview. Maybe it was because the company advertised itself as a company that valued innovation and new ideas. Maybe I could develop my true passion by working there. Maybe I could become a more creative person. There were so many maybes, so many uncertainties. I wasn't even sure if I could be a good accountant when I grew older.

At that point in time, I didn't know what I wanted. All I knew was that I had daydreamt about becoming a writer, and yet I couldn't visualize my future clearly because people said that daydreaming was pointless. But I knew what I didn't want: I didn't want to work at a boring job.

Congratulations on Getting a Job

I SENT OUT THREE RESUMES AND went for three interviews. That was it. I couldn't do the job hunting thing any longer because I didn't even know which company I wanted to work for. If I couldn't be a writer, at least I wanted to be a highly paid accountant. It didn't even matter which firm took me in, as long as it took me in soon. I was growing more anxious and desperate by the day.

I had always thought that good news was exciting and able to lift one's spirits. My good news came to me through a phone call with a private number. It was neither exciting nor uplifting; it was rather depressing.

"Good afternoon. May I speak to William, please?"

I tilted my head back and looked at my phone. Duh, Sherlock, you called my smartphone. Who else would be answering besides William himself?

"Speaking," I replied softly.

"Congratulations, you got the job at our company. When can you come over to sign your employment agreement letter?" said the voice at the end of the line.

I knew it. It was her. It was the emotionless, robotic, zombie secretary of the construction company. My hard work had paid off after all. The congratulation message, however, felt like the absolute voice of death, like a stranger sending condolences to me about a family member who had passed away. It was as though someone had drained all the life force out of a living person and forced the carcass to say those exact words. A robot could've given a more exciting congratulation message than her.

There went my interesting future. I was going to work in a company full of zombies and robots and eventually became one as well. But, I was still willing to accept the offer to work at the company.

Yes, I was *that* desperate.

My Journey Begins

The Office on the Twenty-First Floor

O RIENTATION DAY DURING MY TIME in secondary school and university was like an extra holiday. The cool students skipped it because they had better things to do with their lives. I skipped it to stay at home and mentally prepare for the homework and assignments that would soon drown my life in misery.

Orientation day at my new company wasn't a day I could skip. It was the day to meet new colleagues and top management personnel from other departments. It was the day of first impressions. It was also the day my journey as an accountant began.

I stared blankly at the elevator of the company until the sound of the elevator that reached its designated floor pierced into my eardrums, alerting me of my surroundings. Although there was a crowd around me, there was also an uncomfortable silence. People either stared at their newspapers, smartphones, or the empty space in front of them. No one was talking. Every time the elevator made a "ping" sound, a few people would step out of the elevator, and a new group of people would cram themselves into the elevator. I managed to catch the second elevator, as the first one was already full. My prediction was spot on. The second elevator was crammed with people too. After my first day in that company, I could understand how sardines felt being jammed into a can.

The twenty-first floor was the highest floor in the building. It was also the office of the CEO. Stepping out of the elevator, I was immediately greeted by his secretary. The secretary was a guy with dark skin, wide eyes, and a face that could make even the brightest day felt gloomy. In contrast to the robotic secretary in front of the human resources department, this secretary looked like someone had murdered his entire family; his face portrayed the look of a person seeking vengeance. I quickly signed my name and entered the office through the sliding glass door.

The CEO's office could easily have fit at least twelve of the room I was renting at the time. There was a table made out of what I assumed was Bocote wood, based on its texture. There was also a black leather chair comfortable enough to sit a woman who was eight months pregnant. Behind the chair was a wall made of tinted glass that stretched from the ceiling to the floor, revealing a majestic view of the skyscrapers and tiny houses down below. The ceiling was at least twice as high as the average house ceiling, and works of art spread across the ceiling, creating a sense of calm. The walls surrounding the office were made of dark marble tiles that were flawlessly pieced together one by one, giving the entire office an ambiance of formality.

On the left, there were espresso machines and coffee makers accompanied by assorted desserts. On the right, there was a huge oval table with a podium at the end. It was evident that the right corner of his office was the CEO's meeting room, where he stood on the podium, giving instructions to top management personnel about the company's future. Hung from the right wall were his past achievements over the years. Certificates, pictures, and trophies arranged themselves neatly from the first award he ever received until the most recent award he attained. When I turned around to face the sliding glass door that closed behind me, I saw his gigantic portrait hanging above the door. He was in his formalwear, equipped with a suit and tie, giving out his most sincere smile. To me, the smile looked like the most forceful thing he had ever done. There were three values imprinted below the gigantic portrait. They were "integrity, loyalty, and humility".

As the founder of such a great construction company, he really did live up to his name, and his magnificent office told the world about his success stories. The people who worked with him said that he valued humility and was a humble man.

I was laughing in my mind. He was a humble man all right, as humble as his magnificent office on the twenty-first floor.

A Motivational Speech

THERE WERE ABOUT TEN NEW colleagues who started on the same day as me. Or were there only nine people present? I was too busy scrolling through my phone to avoid making conversation with anyone in the office. I was bad at making small talk or speaking professionally. There was only one thing I was good at, and it was writing.

The exchange of laughter and chit-chat came to a halt when a man walked towards the podium, accompanied by a person who seemed to be his bodyguard. It was the CEO himself, covered in his black blazer, custom made to perfection. In fact, everything he wore looked custom made, including his shirt, his pants, and even his shoes. Under the bright office light, his attire was sparkling. It looked like it had been dipped in glitter.

Besides his perfect attire, his motivational speech was flawless as well. I was moved by his speech, by its contents, and by the way he delivered it to the crowd. He said that it all started with a small guy who had a big dream. He packed all his things into a bag that he carried on his back and left his hometown. He arrived at the city of Kuala Lumpur and started his own construction company. It was his passion for his dream that allowed him to achieve everything he ever wanted. He told us to dream beyond our means and to let our dreams evolve as we grew older. He hoped to give future generations a better life.

He said that the room was filled with dreamers. Whether we were newcomers or existing employees of the company, we must contribute our time and effort for the greater good. Over the ages, the company had built schools, hospitals, and stations for public transport. Every decision made by the company was intended to enhance the well-being of the public. By joining him and his company, we would make the world a better place for our future generations. He ended his speech by saying, "Nature is neutral; if you do the same things that other successful people have done, you will inevitably enjoy the same success they have!"

Working as an accountant at a construction company might not be as horrible as I had imagined it to be. In a way, I was contributing to society like my friend Yap wanted me to do. Besides, if I followed in my CEO's footsteps, perhaps one day I would be as successful as him.

Office or Construction Site?

O N MY SECOND DAY, I waited patiently inside a small discussion room for my supervisor from the human resource department. The whole office was quiet; only the sound of people typing on their keyboards filled up the background. Little did I know I was going to make a decision that would impact my working life forever.

"Hello, you must be William. I am Lynn, your supervisor," said a woman with long, curly hair who held a stack of brown uniforms in her hand. She had life in her words, like the CEO who gave the motivational speech. Otherwise, it was hard to see anything lively around here. Everyone was busy typing away on their computers, laptops, and smartphones.

"Hi, Lynn," I replied softly, so that my voice didn't interrupt others in the office.

"Are you interested to go to the construction site?" She handed me those brown uniforms.

"What? Did I sign up for this? I thought that accountants were supposed to work in the office, not at the construction site," I asked with confusion.

"The human resources team deduced that based on your vibrant personality, you are best suited to be at the construction site compared to the office. Besides, during the interview, you said that you were open to take on new challenges. This is a new challenge, right? The construction site will allow you to learn things on a hands-on basis. In time, you will progress faster than most of the employees at the company. I believe that you can prosper at the construction site, William. You just have to be confident enough to grab the opportunity when it presents itself," she answered almost immediately. It was like she had already expected me to ask that question. I did say that I was open to accept new challenges during the interview. When I said challenges, I meant that I was willing to complete balance sheets, income statements, and other financial statements. It didn't cross my mind that being relocated to the construction site was considered a challenge.

"Well, I ..." I couldn't find the words to express myself.

"I'll give you a day to think about it. Remember: this is a once in a lifetime opportunity." She ended her conversation, grabbed the uniforms, and left the room.

I was left there to think about whether to stay in the office or to go to the construction site. It seemed like she cared about my career path, and she had sincerity in her voice. Perhaps my personality was more suited to working at a construction site. After all, I dreaded the feeling of being trapped in an office. It seemed like going to the construction site was my only option.

After an hour of evaluating the pros and cons of working at the construction site, I felt more confused than ever. I've never worked at a construction site before, but I decided to believe in Lynn's recommendation because she told me that she had my best interest at heart. Eventually, I went to her cubicle and told her that I was ready to go to the construction site. She handed me the uniforms with a smile and said, "I knew you would make the right choice." I was pretty sure I had played directly into her hands.

Nobody Cares

I
T WAS THAT TIME OF year when the sky in Kuala Lumpur was covered with haze. In other countries, they had spring, summer, autumn, and winter. But in Malaysia, specifically Kuala Lumpur, we had summer and the haze season. As Malaysians, we had been blaming the Indonesians for years for conducting open burning. Every year, the same complaints were launched, and every year, nothing changed. It was like they didn't even care.

On my third day of work, the haze was so bad that the schools were forced to close down. Everywhere I went, outdoors or indoors, I smelled smoke, and my skin felt like it was set on fire. It was like the whole of Kuala Lumpur was hosting a huge barbecue party and I was the meat, waiting to be roasted. I was frustrated and sad at the same time. I was frustrated at the haze. I was sad because I had traded the boring lifestyle in Kuala Terengganu, with abundant fresh air and clear water, for a city life filled with cars and haze. I felt like I had made the worst decision ever in my life. I tried to calm myself down but to no avail. Taking in deep breaths was pointless. When I inhaled, I smelled smoke; when I exhaled, I smelled smoke again.

Standing at the front entrance of the company at 6:50 a.m. while waiting for my finance team leader to drive me to my designated construction site wasn't how I pictured my third day of working with the company. In fact, since schools were closed down for the day, weren't companies supposed to close down as well? Oh, that's right; working adults needed money and they were paid only *when* they were working.

The CEO and shareholders were probably on their vacation in the Bahamas or Hawaii, where there were fresh air and water. I was waiting to be transferred to the construction site despite the haze. I imagined the CEO saying, "Employee well-being? What's that? Let's make them work to death!" in his shorts while lying down comfortably on the beach. I hated the fact that I had to work on a day like that, and I felt that companies in Kuala Lumpur weren't concerned about the health of their employees.

The Longest Ride

"ARE YOU WILLIAM?" SAID A lady driving a Suzuki Swift at the front entrance of the company, transferring my thoughts back into reality.

I looked at her and nodded. She tilted her head to look at the passenger seat and stared at me straight in the eyes. I was pretty sure she had gestured me to get into the passenger seat, so I went along with it.

Have you ever been on a fun road trip with your friends and family? Although you were on the road for six to eight hours, you enjoyed every minute of it chatting and laughing with each other. You felt like the hours passed by so fast until suddenly, you arrived at your destination. The trip with my new boss was nothing like that. In fact, it was the complete opposite.

She didn't talk much. Who was I kidding? She hardly talked at all. The whole ride had that awkward, silent atmosphere. And it was a small car. As we sat close to each other, the awkwardness between us became unbearable. I tried to make small talk, but my brain was a total blank. I was seldom lost for words, but at that very moment, I was speechless. Luckily, she turned on her GPS. In that uncomfortable absence of conversation, occasionally the GPS would scream, "In three hundred meters, turn right." Well, at least the GPS wasn't shy to talk.

Drowned out by the deafening silence, and mostly trying to finish my sentences in between the voice of the GPS, I tried to make quick conversation with my new boss. I knew that her name was Shan based on the information I attained from the human resources department, but since she didn't bother introducing herself, it was up to me to ask.

"You are Shan, right?" I said awkwardly. She nodded.

"Nice … erm … car you have there." I tried to smile widely. I could feel the tension on my cheeks. She responded with a mere "hmm" and continued driving.

"You bought the car yourself?" I was already desperate. It wasn't even a good question. She replied with "mmm". All the effort I put into making a decent conversation was rewarded with replies of "hmm" or "mmm". Her replies weren't even a known language, and I was pretty sure that I was speaking in English.

"In one kilometre, turn left and keep right," the GPS gave instructions again. Was I acting in a silent movie? The GPS gave me more responses than my boss, and I didn't even make conversation with the bloody GPS. Talk about being unfriendly! I tried numerous times to create a conversation, but she wouldn't respond. She answered "How do you find working at the construction site?" with a "hmm", not even an "OK". Maybe she was trying to focus on the road, but I gave up. I just sat in the passenger seat, quiet as a mouse.

I was sure she was pressed for time, based on her occasional loud sigh and her "come on!" when we were behind slow drivers. Out of the blue, she would signal to the left or right and immediately make a sharp turn to overtake the slower cars. Sitting in the same car as her was like riding a very fast roller coaster that seemed like it would run out of its tracks at any time, except in roller coaster rides, you hear the sound of people screaming. In her car there was silence, pure silence, and her facial expression didn't change even when she made the sharp turn. The ride to the construction site was supposed to last only an hour, but it was truly the longest ride of my life!

When we finally reached the construction site, she slammed her brakes, and the car came to a sudden stop. I felt the seat belt holding on to me, preventing me from flying out of the windshield. Then she looked at me and took a deep breath.

"William, I apologize for being so quiet. I am just not good at making conversation with strangers." She smiled as we both got out of her car.

For the whole trip, she spoke one sentence, not counting the "come on", "mmm", and "hmm" sounds she made. It was my first day with my new boss, and I was really terrified of her.

Welcome to the Construction Site

WHEN SHAN AND I ARRIVED at the entrance of the construction site, we were greeted by the security guard who was stationed there to ensure that only authorized personnel were allowed into the site. He happily greeted Shan like they were close friends, chatting about the traffic and weather as though I were invisible. When Shan introduced me to him, he handed me the Personal Protection Equipment (PPE), which consisted of a blue plastic helmet, safety boots, and a neon yellow safety vest.

With a strict facial expression, he said, "Welcome to the construction site. It sucks, you will love it!" What had I signed up for? I was doomed!

As the front gate opened and my eyes took in the entire construction site for the first time, I was in tears, but not because I was touched or feeling sad. It was because the cloud of dust had entered my eyes.

In secondary school, I learnt about different kinds of pollution and the effects of pollution on mankind. Beyond the front gate, I experienced all the different kinds of pollution known to man, and they all decided to gather at that construction site. My mind immediately made up a list of things that would potentially ruin my life.

There were a lot of machines towering over the tiny workers at the site, such as the concrete mixers, tower cranes, backhoe loaders, boring machines, and hydraulic breakers. The machines were busy performing their daily duties. Some were digging holes in the ground, and some were crushing rocks. Every machine made loud rumbling noises, each competing to outperform the others. When I was younger, I babysat an annoying baby who cried nonstop, and I felt that my brain exploded inside my head. The construction site was a whole new level of irritation. I felt my internal organs being crushed and vibrated furiously by the loud noises. Sound pollution, check.

As if the haze that filled the sky weren't enough to make my breathing difficult, the construction site was filled with dust and other smelly odours. When I attempted to breathe, my nostrils immediately picked up the sour stench as though a smelly feet was shoved up my nose. From my surroundings, I could see that the air was filled with haze, dust from the crushed rocks, sand particles, the smell of machines emitting diesel fumes, and the sweat of five hundred employees. Air pollution, check.

When I searched for the water dispenser to hopefully get a drink of water to drown away the sour smell in my nose, I was told that the *only* clean water dispenser was the one right beside me near the guardhouse. It looked like it had seen better days. The tap of the water dispenser was broken in half; the drain was clogged with mud, stones and other things that I dared not imagine; and the body was filled with mud lumps, black fingerprints, and shoe marks. My only source of water was from that thing? I would rather die of thirst. Water pollution, check. OK, it was more like water fountain pollution. Get it?

The ground beneath my feet was soft due to the mixture of polymer and earth. When I pressed my feet gently on the ground like a toddler taking his first steps, I felt that the earth was swallowing my feet. With each step I took, my weight became heavier as mud clung tightly to my feet. Walking at the construction site was like playing a real-life game of death. Aside from the nails and steel bars that were sticking out of the ground, designed to kill me if I fell, the path was uneven and filled with potholes, surrounded by even deeper holes that the machines had dug up. Soil pollution, check.

I didn't know which was worse, the fact that working at that construction site would potentially kill me or the fact that I felt like killing myself before I started work. Forget about having a decent salary. With good karma and a lot of luck, I just hoped that I would be able to survive.

Construction Site Guide 101

"**L**ET'S WALK TO THE CABIN where we work." Shan said as she walked casually ahead of me. I was still standing a few feet from the guardhouse in shock.

"You mean that hell hole?" I said with a high-pitched voice, partially yelling to make sure that my statement reached Shan's ears as the machines rumbled ahead of me. She turned her head and smiled at me, assuring me that the whole situation wasn't as bad as I imagined it to be. Then she continued to lead me towards the cabin.

I could swear that everything at the construction site was trying to kill me – the gigantic machines, the slippery slope of soft earth, and, ironically, even the safety equipment I was wearing. The chin strap on my safety helmet wrapped itself around my chin so tightly that I could feel my airways being crushed, as though a person was slowly choking me to death. As I tried to inhale deeply to allow air into my lungs, I felt dust and sand tickling my nostrils, making me sneeze uncontrollably.

Shan was popular at the construction site. She was greeted by many engineers. They were very willing to help her get around the site because she was one of the very few women there. As I observed closer, I realized that Shan and the engineers spoke the same language, except Shan *never* said a single curse word. In contrast, the engineers were crude. They cursed, a lot! Almost every sentence in their speech contained the "F" word. Whether because they had a limited vocabulary or there were no other words to describe the unbearable situation, the "F" word was thrown around in their speech like it was the most natural thing to say. The weird thing was, nobody at the construction site was offended.

Finally, I reached the cabin. Almost immediately, I took off the annoying safety helmet, the boots, and the vest. I felt normal again without the extra weight. When I entered the cabin, I felt like I was entering a small office, with printers and computers positioned strategically to save space. Aside from the mud clumps and the foul stench of sweat, the cabin did felt like an actual office. I was seated in the same room as Shan so that she could keep an eye on me. "This is my workplace now. This is where I will be for the next few years," the inner voice in my head spoke.

Before I could rationalize the nightmare that I was residing in, Shan interrupted me by saying that I should consider taking the train to the nearest station and walking to the construction site. The construction site was situated in the heart of Kuala Lumpur, where traffic was congested twenty-four hours a day. Since I was working in the city, parking lots for cars were very limited, and I had to arrive extra early in order to get a parking spot. Unless I drove a four-wheel-drive car like the Mitsubishi Triton, I couldn't park inside the construction site. Hence, taking the train was the most convenient and economical method.

Suddenly, the morning incident started to make sense. No wonder Shan was driving violently. She needed to fight her way through the traffic to get a parking spot.

Great. I had always wished for a memorable adventure in Kuala Lumpur. Seeing that my first day at the construction site had been filled with surprises and life-threatening encounters, I would definitely have a great story to tell my friends and family. I hoped to live long enough to share my wonderful nightmare.

Dying to Get Out

I T HAD BEEN A WEEK since I started working at the construction site. I wasn't a curious man. Apart from the front entrance to the cabin, the furthest I had explored so far was the portable toilet beside the cabin.

"Come on, William, aren't you excited to tour the site?" Shan invited me. She was determined to drag me along for the "fun" tour. She was very curious about the reason I signed up to work at the construction site, given that I dreaded almost everything there. I wanted to tell her that I was involuntarily convinced to come there, but I chose to remain quiet, since whatever I said wouldn't alter my situation.

"The only thing I am excited about is dying to get out of this hell hole," I replied with a hint of sarcasm. She laughed at me and insisted that I get used to the construction site. Since I didn't want to disappoint her, I tagged along.

The walk around what I thought to be "the graveyard of my dream" was an eye-opening experience. I actually enjoyed it. I learnt about the functions of the operation team and the support team, the different kinds of machines, and their usefulness at the construction site. Apparently, that site was using the top-down construction method to build an underground car park. First, we had to finish the concourse level, and then we would proceed to basement one, two, and three.

Just as I was gazing at the machines digging their way downwards, I tripped and fell on my knees, both of my hands sank into the disgusting mud. I was literally in deep shit, with the mud covering my hands and my jeans. I could already smell myself. I smelled like sweat and crap, mixed together to destroy my day. I knew that walking around the site had been a bad idea. I just knew it. But no, Shan had to talk me into it.

Hearing the sound of me falling, Shan quickly turned her head and stood in front of me. She giggled like a little kid watching a funny cartoon show. "Wow, you are literally *dying* to get out of this hell hole. I know that working yourself to death is a common thing to say nowadays, but this is just too real! Pun intended." She held out one of her hands to help me get up on my feet.

I grabbed her clean hand with both my muddy hands and got up. She was still giggling uncontrollably. Somehow, the situation brightened, and I started laughing as well. Her whole strict-boss figure dissolved away along with our laughter. That was the first time I had seen the funny side of Shan. She was very quick-witted and she was able to ease my difficult situation with a joke. I didn't know whether to feel silly for falling into the mud or feel glad because my boss was a creative person who made funny puns.

After I cleaned myself up, I took a good look in the mirror and laughed at myself again. Yes, I did fall while walking around the site, but nothing was broken, nothing except for my pride. Shan taught me many things that day, but the most important lesson was to learn to laugh at myself, even when something bad happened to me.

At the end of the day, Shan bought Haagen-Dazs ice cream to cheer me up because I had acted like a kid at site. I told her that there was no Haagen-Dazs at site; there were only haze and dust. I also managed to make a pun to cheer myself up.

The Day the World Ended

As I was two weeks at my job, out of the blue, Yap called me during the night, saying that he had graduated from the University of Adelaide and he was returning to Malaysia for good. After the phone call, I began to recall the last time I spoke to him.

Once upon a time, the Mayan civilization predicted that on 21 December 2012, the world as we knew it would come to an end. To make the prediction more realistic, a movie named *2012* was produced to convince the public that the end was upon us. The movie portrayed that meteorites would crash onto the surface of the earth, causing the ground to quake and the ocean to send merciless waves, drowning millions of people.

Believing that the world would end after 2012, many people around me started doing crazy things on their bucket list and spending their hard-earned money on useless junk. The worst part was, even my friend Yap believed that the world was ending. I couldn't understand why a man of science would accept that nonsense. He kept telling me that he wanted to do something meaningful for the less fortunate before his life faded away. In fact, he was so convinced that the world would end that he bet one thousand *Ringgit* with me. I accepted his bet, thinking that if the world didn't end, I would be one thousand *Ringgit* richer; if the world did end, I wouldn't need to pay him anyway. That was by far, my safest bet ever!

As a dentist, Yap insisted to volunteer himself to Africa and provide free oral care for the community. Even if he was rejected, he was determined to be a member of the medical team to provide healthcare for the sick.

As his best friend, it was my duty to convince him that he was out of his mind. I started spreading lies about how he might be eaten alive by wild animals or smuggled into another country as a slave. I realized that I would be going to hell for badmouthing another continent, but I didn't care. I wasn't about to lose my friend just because the world decided to end.

Unfortunately, my efforts were in vain. Yap had already made up his mind to go to Africa. He signed up for a volunteer programme and bought his flight tickets.

He was nuts. I used the words "total bullshit" to describe his insanity. He was the first Malaysian I knew who wanted to go to Africa. I couldn't help but imagine that all those medical textbooks and experiments had driven him mad. He still had his dentistry course to complete, and yet he was willing to put it on hold to help the needy.

As I saw him off to his volunteer programme, I sat at the airport and went through a series of flashbacks, hoping to understand his bold actions.

I realized that Yap was a great man. He had the courage to do what his heart told him to do. He was passionate about his dreams of contributing to society, and he would do his best to fulfil his dreams, regardless of how many people stood in his way. He was truly a brave man with a very big heart.

Just like that, two years had passed. I rarely had the opportunity to chat with him through the phone, but that was about to change.

He was on his way back to Malaysia. Finally, after such a long time, I was going to be reunited with my friend. I was kept awake all night by his exciting news. I couldn't wait to meet him at the airport, and we would definitely have many stories to share.

Who Knew?

THE NEXT EVENING AT 9:00 p.m., I was at the arrival hall of Kuala Lumpur International Airport, frantically searching for a short guy with a big head and curly hair. I was pacing back and forth anxiously, half jumping and half walking as I glanced at every passenger that went through the door of the arrival hall. Yap's flight had arrived at the airport about fifteen minutes ago, but there was no sign of him. He should know how to read the signboards by now. After all, he was an educated adult.

All of a sudden, my eyes zeroed in on a nerd with thick glasses carrying a huge backpack and dragging an oversized luggage. I immediately knew that he was Yap, because no nerd would run towards me screaming my name. The funny part was, I was also screaming his name at the top of my lungs.

Yap told me that his flight back to Kuala Terengganu was at eight thirty the next morning, and he wanted to have a long conversation with me before his next departure. We ended up sitting at McDonalds because it was the only restaurant there that opened for twenty-four hours a day. Before we shared our stories, I had to listen to him nag about how fast food and carbonated drinks could erode my teeth and make me toothless at the age of sixty.

I was chuckling when he used eyes as an analogy to describe our friendship. He said that our friendship was like the eyes on our face:

although we didn't see each other for a very long time, deep down, we knew that we were there for each other. I told him that it was a lousy analogy because eyes could never look at each other unless one of them was dug out from its socket. He laughed and claimed that I was a sadist because apparently "one can look at the mirror to see both of his eyes". Then it hit me, there was no need to dig out my eyes after all.

He shared many exciting encounters while he was volunteering in Africa and how each experience made him realize the importance of healthcare and dental care. As it turned out, the process of helping the less fortunate helped him discover himself. He wanted to expand his horizons by educating Malaysians about the mouth-body connection. He was excited to share the importance of maintaining good oral hygiene and how it would directly improve a person's overall health.

I laughed at his statement because I thought that he was overly naive about his dreams. He took it as a sign of encouragement, and he continued to talk about the various methods of keeping our teeth healthy. We chatted until six in the morning. Many topics were discussed, from political rumours, world events, to ways of making the world a better place.

Just before he boarded his next plane, he handed me a stack of money worth one thousand *Ringgit* and said, "Who knew? The world didn't end after all." I laughed at his silliness, but I didn't take his money.

As Pointless as a Mosquito

A FTER WORKING AT THE CONSTRUCTION site for a month, I was summoned to the headquarters by Lynn for a meeting. She called it a "pulse check session" because it was aimed to check my pulse – you know, to see if I were dead or alive after settling down at that Godforsaken place.

In all seriousness, the session was held to determine my progress as an employee for the company.

The session lasted for an hour. Every minute of it was unbearable. It wasn't like the one-hour-in-the-car-without-talking-to-your-boss kind of unbearable. I was receiving insults from a person I barely knew, and I felt helpless because I couldn't defend myself. It was as though I was a mute person in a courtroom, being found guilty of a crime I didn't commit, and I couldn't speak up to prove my innocence. I left the meeting room more devastated than ever. After the session, I was deprived of all motivation to work, and I sat at my cubicle like a living corpse while staring at the black screen of my laptop.

I thought that in order to find out about a person's well-being, you asked questions and allowed him to provide you with answers. The pulse check session was nothing like that. I listened to her speech about how I wasn't doing enough because I found myself struggling to adapt to a new environment and how I wasn't fond of taking up new challenges because I was afraid of exploring the construction site to gain experiences.

Sometimes, I wondered why mosquitoes exist. Their existence on this planet is pointless except as an alternative food source to another species. I was comparing the useless pulse check session to a mosquito because: number one, it was very annoying, and my ears were tired of listening to Lynn pointing out my flaws as if I hadn't already seen them, just like a mosquito buzzing loudly beside my ears. Number two, it was energy draining. I left the room feeling so down that I could hardly get any work done that day, exactly as if a million mosquitoes had drained away all my blood and left my lifeless body in front of a laptop. Number three, mosquitoes served as a food source for other animals, and that meeting was done solely for the benefit of others. The session didn't help me solve any of my problems. It was done so that Lynn could report to the top management team that she had done her job of checking up on the new employee, which would eventually boost her performance as a human resources manager. Typical human resources personnel.

I was in so much rage that day. If that was what it took to be a human resources supervisor, I could've easily done her job with my eyes closed! How hard was it to allow a person to give feedback about his condition? A pet could've done a better job than her! I thought it was common sense that to care for another person, it was important to allow a safe space for him to share his feelings instead of enforcing opinions on him. Perhaps I might gain some insights by listening to his perspective for once. At the very least, he wouldn't go home and rage about me in his journals.

A Boss with a Special Power

IN CONTRAST TO LYNN, I realized that Shan had a special power.
She could read minds!

Just kidding. If you called the ability to make friends a special
power, then Shan would be qualified as a superhero. She was a simple
person. However, she understood people at a deep level. She listened
attentively to what people had to say, and above all else, she listened
to what people didn't say.

After months of working at the construction site, I noticed that
the finance corner of the cabin was also the counselling corner.
Many employees came to tell Shan about their problems, whether
they were work-related or life-related. They always ended up feeling
comforted after talking to her.

Have you ever heard of the saying, "Don't listen to reply, but
listen to understand"? Knowing the quote was easy; applying it
in real life was a whole different story. Amazingly, Shan was able
to relate to the engineers better than anyone. She could pinpoint
what was truly important among all the curse words they used. She
showed me that one could be friends with others, even if they were
from different backgrounds.

Maybe it was just my imagination, but I felt that the engineers
loathed me. I was commonly greeted with, "Aren't you an accountant?
Why are you here?" or "I don't think you can last another day here".

Even after months of working there, they still wouldn't accept me. I knew that I couldn't be one of them, but their words still hurt me deeply. Shan would usually play the role of a big sister who consoled me after listening to their hurtful remarks.

To make me feel better, she said that the long hours of working under the sun had fried most of their brain cells, causing them to be angry about everyone and everything in their lives. Once I got to know them, I would see that they were very straightforward. They never sugar-coat their sentences and said what they want without thinking about the feelings of others. They would tell me my flaws as they were, and it was up to me to improve myself.

Just as she understood the engineers, Shan understood me as well. I had the feeling that she knew I wasn't very enthusiastic about staying at the construction site. She knew how much it hurt me when I was placed in a foreign environment and consistently underestimated by the people who worked there. Her words of encouragement and undying belief that I could be better always helped me to be more positive despite the harsh environment.

To hear words of encouragement during work was very important to me. I had always wanted to grow stronger, and I wanted to be tougher too, not just for the colleagues who worked at the site, but for myself. That was the reason I left my hometown in the first place.

I would be working at the construction site for a very long time. I wanted to adapt to my new environment, and I wanted to thrive in it.

Hanging Out with Engineers

V ERY OFTEN, I WOULD START daydreaming after work while I walked from the cabin towards the entrance of the construction site. It was a five-minute walk, and my mind had plenty of time to wander off into fantasy land.

One night, before I reached the front entrance, greetings from the engineers on duty snapped me back into reality. They were discussing about supper because they were planning to stay at the construction site throughout the night to monitor the casting of floor slabs. One of the engineers casually put his arm on my shoulder and invited me to join them for supper. Seeing that they were muscular engineers and I was just a pale, skinny accountant, and mainly because I imagined that they could easily snap my neck if I rejected their offer, I agreed to tag along for supper.

It was already 10:00 p.m., and I would definitely miss the last train home. But as a person who didn't have many friends, I decided to give that random encounter a chance to foster a bond with the engineers. I was desperate for their approval.

Besides, Shan convinced me that I should give myself a chance to get to know the engineers better by attending lunch or dinner sessions together. Once I got to know them, I would understand that they weren't scary people. They were all bark and no bite. If I could tolerate all their cursing, perhaps a beautiful friendship could bloom.

The conversations during supper were very interesting. I thought that engineers were mostly realists, but the engineers at the company were absolute pessimists! When something good happened in their lives, they highlighted the negative side.

For instance, an engineer's wife had just given birth to a baby boy. Normally, that would be a happy occasion, but according to him, it meant that there would be an extra mouth to feed. His family would have to incur more expenses, considering the price hikes for milk powder and baby food. He would have more sleepless nights because the baby would cry all night, which consequently forced him to blow his brains out.

On the other hand, the engineer who was about to go on a holiday trip with his girlfriend already imagined that his girlfriend would go on a shopping rampage and swipe his credit card like a madwoman. The overpriced food and wine at the hotel would burn away his hard-earned fortune, and when he finally returned from his horrible trip, he would be as broke as a beggar on the street and eat leftovers for the rest of his miserable life.

Their stories were blown out of proportion. They had such great imaginations. After years of working late at the construction site, their important source of entertainment was storytelling with exaggerated hand gestures and animated tones. As the third party who listened to their stories for the first time, it was hilarious.

Most of the time, I was trying to hold in my laughter, but at some point, I burst out laughing like a little kid. They joined in with their laugher as well. They were also chuckling at each other's misfortune. Although our actions attracted angry gazes from other customers in the food stall, we didn't care; it was a humorous occasion, and we were enjoying our interesting supper.

After supper, one of the engineers offered to drive me home. I spent an additional hour in the car, listening to him rant on about his miserable life experiences and claim that working at his terrible job made him feel like killing himself. When he asked me whether I thought of killing myself after working at the site, I laughed at his question.

It was cruel for me to say, but after listening to his depressing stories, I felt better about my life. Compared to his, my life didn't suck that bad after all.

Home Is Where the Daydream Is

As I got more acquainted with my job, my responsibilities grew. More responsibilities meant more work, and more work meant that I needed to stay longer at the construction site.

It was a huge joke when I read the e-mail sent by the human resource department encouraging employees to maintain work-life balance. There was no work-life balance, only work-life integration.

The tiny clock at the bottom right of my laptop indicated that it was already ten at night, and yet I was staring at my Excel sheet with an empty mind. I decided to stay back and familiarize myself with the task assigned to me. Unfortunately, I didn't get much work done, mainly because the machines were making so much noise that it seemed as though they were having a party. I could hardly focus on anything!

The boring machine was digging deep into the ground, struggling to grind through the limestone that blocked its path. The rotors inside the generators were spinning rapidly to generate electricity for all the spotlights at the construction site. The concrete mixer trucks were lining up at the entrance, each truck waiting for its turn to pour concrete on the ground to cast a floor slab. Whenever I tried to focus on my work, I felt like there was an invisible woodpecker on my head, hammering its beak on my forehead. The irritating noise was hitting on my eardrums so loudly that my ears could no longer function properly.

In the city, there was no difference between night and day. Neon lights brightened every corner of the street. Skyscrapers stretched out to reach the sky, filled with white florescent lights as they surrounded the construction site. Forget about seeing stars, sometimes I couldn't even find the moon.

Kuala Terengganu was very different from Kuala Lumpur. Before I came to the city, everything and everyone had curfew. When the clock struck eleven at night, darkness would consume the land, and the whole place ceased to make a sound. Sometimes I would light up a matchstick just to hear the sound of fire eating away the skinny matchstick. I would often sit on the porch, look up at the pitch-black sky decorated by little shining stars, and imagine that a wall of stars was crashing down on me. Imagining unrealistic adventures used to be fun. I could see my fantasies come alive in my head.

I missed Kuala Terengganu and its quietness at night, but there I was at the construction site working on my Excel sheet. Something had to be done. "You know what? Screw work. I am going back to KT to have a break!" I thought out loud as I applied for my first annual leave to go back to Kuala Terengganu. I could use the break. Besides, it had been a while since I had met up with my friends from home.

Walking Down Memory Lane

T HERE IS A PLACE IN Kuala Terengganu called Chinatown. OK, who am I kidding? Chinatown is an overstatement. There are two rows of traditional Chinese buildings parallel to one another, with a mixture of residential houses and shop houses along the busy street. That's it. There is no Chinatown. There is only a China street.

I liked to take a long stroll along Chinatown, eyeing the tourists who went "oohh" and "aahh" at the murals on the walls of each building. They were busy making funny poses and taking pictures of the splendid works of art. I bet that they didn't know it was an artist named Ping who painted the wonderful murals on the walls. My mind slowly wandered off into the past, when I was about to travel to Kuala Lumpur to search for job opportunities.

Ping had been my friend since high school. She had an undying passion for art. During high school, she had already started to showcase her talents as an artist by beautifying the school scenery. She redecorated the school pond and planted trees and flowers along the walkway from the front entrance to the classrooms inside the school compound. According to her, anything that looked bare and empty was "just asking to be decorated". She was the kind of person who had her whole life figured out, and everything she did brought her a step closer towards her dream. She formed her own company when she was twenty-one years old. The company did almost everything related to art, from designing menus for restaurants, painting murals on walls to organizing weddings for the locals in Kuala Terengganu. She claimed Chinatown as her canvas, and she was dedicated to making the place vibrant and beautiful for the whole world to see.

I also had an undying passion. My creativity came in the form of writing interesting stories to be shared with the world. In contrast to Ping, I was a coward. I dared not pursue my dream because I was afraid of failing. I was so frightened by the thought of failing as a writer and becoming jobless that I banished my dream into the deepest and darkest part of my mind.

I naively assumed that my understanding of mathematics would land me a great career in the business world. Hence, I chose what I thought to be the safest path in my career: to become an accountant. When the economy was booming, companies would need accountants to expand their businesses. When the economy was declining, companies would need accountants to save their businesses. I was sure that I would never be jobless for the rest of my life.

A few days before I departed to Kuala Lumpur as an accountant, I decided to meet up with Ping, desperately hoping that she would give me a solution to maintain my job while pursuing my dream. After she dealt out a huge amount of sass and funny statements on how I would become a working zombie like the people in Kuala Lumpur, her only advice to me was, "you should quit your job".

Even before I began my first job, she was already advising me to quit. If there were a competition about being unsupportive, Ping would win the grand prize. If I were to pursue my passion in the field of arts, would she give me her blessing and support instead? I guessed I would never know, since I stubbornly insisted on becoming an accountant.

Joking and sarcasm aside, she assured me that I was born to do great things, not sit inside a cubicle, staring at Excel sheets on a laptop all day. She used the term "YOLO" (You Only Live Once) to urge me to become a writer. After all, why would I want to spend my life doing something I hate?

Her words had a way of making me reflect on my decisions. I wanted to be a writer, to take the road less travelled, and to pursue the things I was passionate about. Unfortunately, dreaming about becoming a writer wasn't practical. It wouldn't help me make a living. I must face the harsh reality rather than seeking refuge in my fantasy world.

During my final day in Kuala Terengganu, she sent me to the airport. Just before I passed through the departure gate, she yelled, "When you resign, call me. We shall celebrate that auspicious day!" as she waved good-bye. I waved and smiled forcefully.

Just you wait and see, Ping. If I ever resigned, it would mean that I was finally brave enough to chase my dream. Of course I would call her. I would rub my success in her face so hard that she would feel sorry for ever being sarcastic to me.

Hating Something
with Passion

AFTER MY RELAXING STROLL ALONG Chinatown, daydreaming about my past, Ping and I rendezvoused at Old Town White Coffee to catch up on our latest happenings.

"Eww! Your coffee tastes like shit!" She said, right after taking a small sip of my coffee.

I giggled as I watched her frantically pulling a wet tissue out of her handbag and licking it in disgust. I would like to clarify that I wasn't a sadist who enjoyed watching a friend suffer, but my relationship with Ping was a very weird one and often unacceptable to others. Our friendship was built upon the foundation of insults and sarcasm, and we took pleasure in watching the misfortunes that befell each other. With friends like her, who needed enemies?

Once, she dated an immature guy who liked to drink milk. I didn't know which part was funnier, the fact that he liked to drink milk, a lot, or that he had the IQ of a little child whenever we were discussing something serious. Every time we dined at a coffee shop, I would intentionally order milk and mimic that guy's childish behaviour just to get on her nerves. Similarly, when I did something silly in my life, she would happily highlight all my mistakes and consistently remind me of my shame.

As an artist, Ping did everything with great passion, including hating the colour brown. I had never seen anyone who disapproved of the colour brown as deeply as she did. Since the beginning of time, brown was the boringest colour of all boring colours, and boringest wasn't even a word. It was made up solely to address the colour brown. Everything that was boring in her life was brown: brown rice, brown sugar, brown bread. She insisted that brown only existed to make other colours more vibrant, like the tree bark that was unnoticed because people were busy admiring the flowers and the fruits that grew on the trees. Every beverage that was brown surely tasted like shit, including the award-winning overpriced coffee that was right in front of her.

"William, did you know that everything that is brown is potentially hazardous to your health? I mean, look at Chris Brown, for example. His rap is so bad that it burns your ears, and he assaults other people when he is angry. See? Like I said, brown is bad for your health. Stay away from anything that is brown, got it?" Ping gave her opinion with pure confidence.

My giggles quickly transformed into laughter. I was surprised that she could relate Chris Brown to the colour brown. The fun part of having an artistic friend like Ping was that I could never guess what she was thinking.

To drive her further up the wall, I did the unthinkable. I told her that my work uniform was brown.

Immediately, she tilted her head backwards and stared at me in disbelief before putting her palm to her face. "No! Resign. Just … resign. Hell, I would even type the letter for you. All you need to do is sign it," she said with a serious tone.

"That's a lousy and ridiculous reason to resign, don't you think? What am I going to write in my resignation letter? 'Dear employer, I severely dislike the brown uniforms. Hence, this is my notice of resignation,'" I defended myself, thinking that she had gone mad from inhaling too much paint.

"It is a good reason as any. And if they don't understand it, they are not artists." She said it as though it was a common sense.

Ping was the kind of person who disliked things for the oddest reasons. Once, she complained that the fuel indicator in cars was misleading. The "F" meant "full" and the "E" meant "empty". But one might think that "F" meant "finish" and "E" meant "enough". Odd, right?

"You are crazy! Even I don't understand your reason. Did your brains malfunction again?" I jokingly insulted her.

"Am I crazy? Am I? Am I? Or has your employer managed to corrupt your mind? Mark my words, William. After a few months, you will be walking around in that brown uniform saying, 'Brains ... brains'. By that time, it will be too late to save your sorry ass," she hurled another insult back at my face.

That day, we had a great time being mean to one another, joking about each other's misfortunes, and laughing at our own silliness. Before we knew it, the owner of the coffee shop was urging us to leave because he needed to close his shop for the day.

After I went home, I replayed our conversation in my stream of thoughts. A part of me realized that my strong defence against her insults wasn't because I was fond of my brown uniforms. It was because she was right about my feelings when I worked in that company. I was always burdened with work, and my life was slowly transforming into a dull routine. Much like the colour brown, my life was no longer vibrant.

Tips to Keep Your
Teeth Healthy

DURING MY BREAK IN KUALA Terengganu, I also had the
opportunity to catch up with Yap.

I wouldn't say that I am a normal person. What is normal, anyway? As Charles Addams once said, "Normal is just an illusion. What is normal for the spider is chaos for the fly".

On the other hand, I wouldn't say that I am a freak either. If there were a label for a person who is somewhere in between, I would categorize myself as that label. I admit that I am a person with weird personalities. I like to be alone most of the time, and I indulge in daydreaming. Consequently, I make friends with weird people as well. You know what they say, "birds of a feather flock together".

Speaking of having weird friends, if you happened to stumble across a guy who shoved a straw way too deep down his throat just to get a drink, congratulations! You had officially found my friend Yap, The best part was, he did it on purpose.

I had been staring at his actions for a while now, but he continued to sip his drink with difficulty, as the straw was too deep into his mouth. I waited for him to explain what the hell was he doing, but he thought that it was natural to drink his beverage that way. He was also the same person who didn't rinse his mouth after brushing his teeth because apparently, toothpaste contained fluoride which would strengthen his teeth.

"May I ask what in the name of heavens are you doing with your straw?" I tapped on my glass and mimicked his weird action.

"Oh. This?" He continued to sip his drink.

"Well …" I was waiting for an answer. He was a dentist, after all. I was hoping that there would be a scientific explanation for his actions. Then again, he was also the same person who believed that the world would end on 21 December 2012. Yap was always full of surprises. Sometimes I had a hard time keeping up with his shenanigans, but that was the beauty of having such a great friend. Life would never be boring when he was around.

"I am trying to protect my teeth, you see. Do you know that the enamel of our tooth starts to demineralize at pH 5.5? Yes, although our saliva contains calcium and phosphate ions, which help to slow down the process, the drinks that we drink play an important role too. For example, the lemonade that I am drinking ranges from pH 2.5 to 3.0. Since it is not good for my teeth, I choose to put the straw deep into my throat so that when I drink the lemonade, it won't have any contact with my teeth." He explained confidently, like a lecturer conducting a class.

"What?" I was stunned. Our get-together session had been quickly transformed into an educational lecture on oral care.

He ended up spending the entire evening educating me, talking about the causes and effects of plaque build-up and the ways to prevent gingivitis. He aimed to save every tooth and believed that tooth extraction should only be done as a last resort. Furthermore, he played a video of his lecturer extracting a wisdom tooth from her patient. It was bloodier than I imagined it to be but not unpleasant to Yap. He *loves* teeth.

I learnt a thing or two about oral care after talking to Yap. He was so passionate about his job and what he did on a daily basis that he needed to share his knowledge with someone. To the majority of the people I knew, he was a nerd who was obsessed with oral health, but I was happy to have an awesome friend like him.

The Red Flag

I HATE SURPRISES. IN MY ENTIRE life, I have had only a few surprises, but none of them has ever ended well.

When I was seven years old, I was watching cartoons in my living room, and I received a phone call from the hospital. The nurse wanted to speak to my parents because my grandmother had passed away. Minutes later, I was at the hospital crying, and my parents were busy planning a funeral.

When I was fifteen years old, I saw my mother tearing up by herself in her room. I asked her what happened, and she told me that our beloved dog managed to enter into our neighbour's compound. Thinking that it was a wolf, my neighbour put a bullet straight through its head. I didn't recall ever seeing a wolf in Kuala Terengganu.

After I returned to work from my holiday, I checked my inbox and saw a red flag on one of my e-mails. That was definitely not a good surprise. The e-mail was sent to me by an unknown person demanding that I prepare the requested financial statements for audit purposes. Then it dawned upon me that the auditors were coming to the construction site. The e-mail was sent to me two days ago, which meant that I had three more days until they arrived. Why did they have to send me the e-mail during my holidays? Didn't they know the term "bad timing"? I read through the e-mail slowly, hoping that it was just a nightmare and I would miraculously wake up, but it was reality, and a harsh one. At the end of the e-mail, there was a statement saying "thank you for your cooperation", which made me feel even more uncomfortable.

Are they joking? That wasn't how cooperation worked. I didn't sign up for this. I didn't sign up for *any* of this. Why did the auditors have to do things at the last minute? Couldn't they plan ahead of time instead of sending me the e-mail with a red flag?

I hated the auditors for sending the urgent e-mail. To be more precise, I hated the red flag that was attached to the left side of the e-mail icon. It signified that there was an uphill task waiting for me, and most of the time, it would be impossible to complete it within the deadline. I let out a huge sigh. There was no point in complaining about the red flag. I must get back to work soon.

Shan seemed to be accepting the e-mail rather positively, rushing back and forth, making phone calls to the headquarters to retrieve the financial documents. By evening, the already crowded little cabin was a total chaos, with heavy boxes everywhere and documents on our tables. While sorting through the dust-filled documents, Shan said, "Sometimes, I really hate the auditors. They make our lives miserable. That is why I quit my previous job as an auditor." She smiled wearily.

She told me that for every cloud there is a silver lining. She claimed that with a positive attitude and the help of an assistant, she had already won half the battle. Even the most difficult task could be made easy with a positive attitude. Then she joked about the need to be positive, especially at the construction site, or else I would end up like the engineers, who often complained about the issues that happened in their lives. Despite the constant sneezing due to the dust, at least we had fun sorting out the documents.

Well, I guessed that I would have to spend most of my time retrieving documents and arranging them nicely for the auditors. At least I wasn't alone. I had Shan to keep me company. I looked forward to learning from that unforgettable experience. See what I did there? I tried to be positive in a desperate situation.

Problems and Solutions

WORKING AT THE CONSTRUCTION SITE was like reading a mathematics book that was full of problems. Whereas a mathematics book gave me the answers at the end of the book, at the construction site, if I couldn't solve a problem, it will be the end of me.

You know, I never asked for a problem. It just decided to invite itself unknowingly into my life without my permission. The worst part was, I needed to solve it. On top of having to prepare the documents for the auditors, I was burdened with random challenges that happened at the construction site.

I came to work early in the morning and saw an e-mail from an engineer stating, "Dear William, can you please find out the reasons why are we not paying our suppliers? They stopped the supply of concrete, and I need to cast the floor slab soon. Thank you!" I just stared at the screen, wondering how in the name of heavens I could find out the answer to that question. But he demanded an answer, a solution that would ease his troubles. It was up to me to solve the problem. I called the suppliers, bankers, and creditors to find out what had caused the delay of payment.

I told Shan that every time the office phone rang and it displayed an external number, my heart would skip a beat. It was always bad news, and it was driving me mad, slowly but surely. The creditors called to ask for payment. The debtors called to ask for certified true copies of documents in order for them to make payment. The bankers called to tell me that the online banking system was under maintenance and they couldn't process my payment. Problem after problem piled up in my head, and I had a hard time solving them because most of the problems were out of my control. I liked to have control over things, just like I could control my imagination.

As I was ranting about the issues I encountered, I noticed that Shan observed me in amazement as she rested her hands on her chin, like a mother watching her own kid throwing a tantrum around the house. She was always calm and collected when she dealt with my issues. None of them ever gave her too much excitement or made her overly sad. Sometimes I wondered what was going on inside that head of hers while she was listening to my complaints.

"The thing about life is, everything is balance," she started her speech.

"What? Have you been listening to me? What do the problems I faced have to do with balance?" I interrupted her.

She chuckled softly. Deep inside her head, she must have thought that I was acting like a child who only knew how to complain. "As I was saying, everything in life is balanced. Problems exist for us so that we can find solutions, and to find solutions, we must first solve the problems. One cannot exist without the other. We should see problems as a gift, not a curse. Every problem that we solve strengthens us to face future challenges. Only by solving more problems do we become strong and move forward. That is how we can be successful in life. So, William, stay positive. I am sure you can solve all your problems and emerge victorious." Shan seldom talked. When she finally said something, it was usually very profound. I was amazed at how she analyzed my problems, but I wanted to be cheeky about my reply.

"So, in the end, it is still up to me to solve the problems, right?" I said the sentence after a long sigh.

"Yup," she nodded, knowing that I couldn't escape from my responsibilities even if I wanted to. We both had a good laugh at my predicament.

I was very impressed with Shan. Beneath her cool expression, she was very wise at giving advice, especially to a difficult person like me. No matter how difficult a situation was, after she advised me, it seemed like the problems faded into nothingness.

From our conversation, I realized something. I still had much to learn from her.

SLEEP

MY ONE-HOUR LUNCH TIME WAS shortened to thirty minutes, mainly because I couldn't keep my eyes open to eat my tasteless meal. Bad food aside, I had been working long hours, and my sleep at night was interrupted by the beeping sound of incoming messages on my phone. It was only natural for me to feel sleepy during my lunch hour. I decided to sink into the big office chair, put on a pair of headphones, and register myself in dreamland.

There were many things that I had woken up to in my life. One was the sound of birds chirping in the morning. Another was the sensation of freezing cold water thrown on my face by my brother so that my morning would be "more refreshing". The worst of them all was my boss staring at me with her eyes wide open in shock.

Waking up to Shan standing in front of me with her eyes fixed on the little stunt I had just pulled, I jumped up immediately and accidentally pushed my chair backwards, almost falling off it. My mind quickly came up with an excuse to explain my situation, and I blurted out, "Erm, I was just doing the Stress Level Elimination Exercise Plan (SLEEP), the training that the human resources team sent me to last month."

I leaned my head backward and laughed loudly. It was exaggerated and I knew it, but I didn't care. I was lying. There was no Stress Level Elimination Exercise Plan. I had read about it online as a good excuse to give to my boss when I was caught dozing off during work. I hoped that somehow Shan would buy into my lies after looking at my forceful laughter.

Instead of feeling upset, she quickly countered my statement with, "Why don't you say that you left the cap of the glue open and you accidentally took in too many whiffs and fainted?" There was a pregnant pause, and eventually both of us giggled maniacally.

Shan assured me that we are humans after all, sometimes we would feel tired. Consequently, she taught me her secret technique of staying awake during work. Whenever she felt sleepy, she would excuse herself to the restroom due to an "uncomfortable sensation" in her stomach. Then, she would take a short nap in the restroom or wash her face excessively to stay awake. Alternatively, she would go to the emergency staircase to take forty winks. The staircase method was a bit risky because colleagues who smoked at that location could definitely catch her dozing off during work.

Thanks to my creative boss, I learnt the ways of napping at work. Bosses like her were very hard to come by. She was never rigid or uptight towards her subordinates. Instead of pinpointing my mistakes, she understood the difficulties that I needed to endure and treated me with compassion. She was truly a great boss whom I respected with all my heart.

I never thought that I would say it, but I was starting to see Shan as a good friend. As it turned out, it wasn't impossible to discover new friends at work after all.

Applying My Medical Leave

A S PING ONCE SAID, "No one dies a virgin, because life screws us up one way or another." Actually, she used the "F" word rather than "screws".

After days of burning the midnight oil to prepare documents for the auditors, I was exhausted. I spent every day preparing the purchase orders, delivery orders, and material requisition orders so that when the auditors came to the construction site, they would have an easy access to all the important documents. It had been a while since I had managed to see the sun. I woke up in the morning at five thirty to go to work and returned home at midnight or later. The only silver lining was that I had one more stack of documents to sort out and I would finally complete my task.

I had the day all planned out. My aim was to finish my task before six in the evening and go to bed early, but life had something more exciting in store for me.

I was exhausted from working late the previous night. As a result, I had forgotten to charge my phone, and the battery decided to die just before my alarm could go off. I managed to jump out of bed at seven in the morning when the first sun ray touched my face. I needed to take a quick shower to freshen up my sleepy face, so I dashed like a madman into the bathroom, forgetting to turn on the water heater. When the stream of ice-cold water hit the top of my head, I realized that despite being a twenty-four-year-old adult, I could still scream like a six-year-old girl who got frightened.

After getting dressed, I looked at the clock in the living room because my trusty smartphone had died on me. It was ten past seven. I could still make it to work before eight if I drove like a lunatic.

I had never been late to work before, and that day wasn't going to be my record-breaking day. But seriously, what was I thinking? I was living in Kuala Lumpur. Of course there was traffic congestion. That day, a few cars had overheated and broken down in the middle of the road, worsening the congestion. I stared at the clock inside my car. It was seven thirty. Still hoping to reach work on time, I continued driving dangerously.

Then I saw something that shattered my hopes of arriving to work on time. The fuel icon was blinking nonstop in front of my eyes. Pumping petrol into my car would delay my traveling time, making me late for work. But since cars couldn't function without fuel, my only option was to drive to the nearest petrol station.

I slammed my hands against the steering wheel, yelling the "F" word as loud as I could. I knew that I was rude, but I couldn't care less. I *was* late for work. So, I drove back home, plugged my phone into its charger, and called Shan. I did what I had to do: I faked that I had a severe headache with cough and flu.

Furthermore, I needed a medical certificate to strengthen my lies. Not only did I need to lie to my boss, I needed to lie to a doctor as well. And what better way was there to lie to a doctor than seeking help from a friend with medical experience?

I called Yap and explained my day. I needed a disease that could land me a medical certificate from a doctor although I was perfectly healthy. He reluctantly advised me to pretend that I had a severe migraine and I felt like my world was spinning, which caused me to feel nauseated every time I tried to focus.

I couldn't believe that my lies actually worked. The doctor gave me some medication and a medical certificate stating that I was unfit for work for a day. The medication cost me fifty *Ringgit*, but who cared? Desperate times called for desperate measures.

I drove home with an uncomfortable feeling, lay in my bed, and began pouring out all my emotions into my journal.

I felt awful for lying to my boss just to take a day off. That day, I felt like my life was screwed up in every way possible.

The Forty-Forty Rule

AFTER A HECTIC WEEK WITH the auditors, Shan and I decided to go to a nice restaurant with the engineers to reward ourselves for our hard work. While walking towards the restaurant, Shan and I discussed the reasons why we enjoyed dining with the engineers. It came to my attention that both of us had one similarity. We were cruel and pathetic accountants who enjoyed preying on other people's misery just to feel better about our lives.

The lunch topic was about the award-giving ceremony for employees who had dedicated their effort to the company for a long period of time. Employees who worked for the company were rewarded for their loyalty. There were four categories in total: ten years, twenty years, thirty years, and forty years. Employees who fell into each category would receive gifts as a token of appreciation from the CEO himself. The most interesting part was, an employee who committed forty years of his life working at the company received some gold coins and the CEO's signature on a certificate stating "Thank you for your commitment and excellent performance".

I was taken aback by the ceremony. After all those years of service at the stressful and blood-sucking company, all he got was a certificate and some gold coins? Not even a freaking Rolex? At least he could've sold off the Rolex to earn a lucrative income.

The engineers advised youngsters like Shan and me to do the things we truly loved, not follow the forty-forty rule that was laid out by the company. It was a huge trap.

An average employee spent forty hours of his life every week working for the company, and he worked for forty years just to get a certificate and some gold coins. When he finally retired, he would live out the rest of his miserable life regretting that he had made the company rich at the cost of his own health and wealth.

To make the situation less depressing, I put forth a positive quote on life, "when life gives you lemons, make lemonade". As a realist, Shan questioned the logic of drinking acidic beverages. One of the engineers responded to the quote from a more bitter perspective. "When life gives you lemons, get angry! Get very, very angry! Claim that you requested oranges and *not* lemons. Demand to see life's manager because he can't get a simple order correct. Make life's manager rue the day for giving you lemons. Then proceed to threaten him by saying you are an engineer, and you aren't afraid to invent a combustible weapon using the lemons to burn his freaking house down. After that, use the weapon of mass destruction to blow up the world!"

The engineers were definitely a creative bunch. I often wondered what was wrong with them and their silly ideas of blowing up the world.

The thing that sparked my curiosity was the reason that they stayed behind and worked for the company although they hated mostly everything about it. I guessed I would never know until I had worked for forty years.

The Day I Became a Monster

THE ENGINEERS HAD A SAYING, "all work and no play makes you a productive employee". Seeing as we worked our youth away at the company, the CEO organized a dinner party for all the staff as a reward, but I had another unexpected event in store for me. My parents made a surprise visit to Kuala Lumpur to see me.

After work, I waved good-bye to my colleagues, who were carpooling to the dinner party. I knew that I couldn't go. Parents were more important than a silly party, right?

No! I wanted to attend the dinner party. It was organized once every year for all the staff of the company. There were supposed to be expensive wine and delicious food, accompanied by the laughter of drunken colleagues.

I would enjoy the company of drunken colleagues. Only when they were drunk enough did they speak the truth and do what they were afraid to do when they were sober. It was my chance to be drunk as well and to socialize with colleagues who worked at other construction sites. Seeing that the engineers at the same construction site as me had a miserable time working there, I wanted to know what it was like working at other construction sites. I really wanted to go to the party.

Timing was everything, and my life was a series of bad timing. It just so happened that the CEO chose that day to organize the dinner party, and my family members decided to pay me a surprise visit on the same day. There were 365 days in a year, and yet two of the important events managed to collide against one another. What were the odds?

I was a busy man, working day and night to complete my tasks, but I wasn't doing enough to please Lynn from the human resources department. She urged me to take on more challenges to boost my career development.

Attending an annual dinner party was a rare occasion. If I wanted to sacrifice my only chance of attending the party, it must be for an important meeting or work-related issues. At least those would help me build a brighter career path. I was only willing to sacrifice such an important event if I had work to do. I wasn't pleased to forgo the dinner party just so I could meet my parents.

The train ride to meet my parents at the mall nearby was like travelling through the Sahara Desert. Sweat was gathering all over my body. Every part of my skin was burning, and I felt that a huge force was pressing against my temples, giving me the worst headache I had ever experienced. My heart was pounding with hatred as though a fiery pit of hell was about to break loose and all the lava came flowing out of my entire body.

I hated my parents. I hated them for their surprise visit. I lived with them for twenty-four years, and yet they didn't know that I loathed surprises. It was my one day to enjoy myself, but they managed to ruin it for me. They could've called a week ahead to schedule an appropriate date before coming to visit me. Was it that difficult to plan ahead? We lived in the era of smartphones, for crying out loud! Why couldn't they just pick up their stupid phones and call me in advance? It would only take a few minutes of our time to avoid these major events from colliding.

I was angry with my entire family. I knew that it was my mother who planned the surprise visit. She played the mom card on me, saying that after I left to work in Kuala Lumpur, I rarely called to bond with her. On the other hand, my dad was a wimp. After years of marriage, he was still the coward he had been before marrying my mother. He dared not object to any of her decisions. I despised my brother for being irresponsible. He should've been a better son to the family, so that my parents would focus their attention on him instead of me.

When I met my parents, I gave them hell. I blamed them for ruining my day, for ruining my life, for ruining everything that mattered to me. I was furious with them. Anger was written across my face. I told them off for every little thing that they did wrong that day. For some unknown reason, they tolerated all my hurtful words that evening.

When I was finally calm, I realized that I had changed. I had changed into a monster, the kind that would sacrifice spending time with his family in order to get drunk with his bosses and colleagues on a Friday night.

After less than a year of working at the company, I was already losing myself. What had happened to me?

The Hunger Games

WHEN THE END OF THE year was just around the corner, my friends were busy preparing their New Year resolutions. I, on the other hand, was busy preparing my employee evaluation form.

Lynn scheduled a meeting to discuss my performance at the company throughout the year. Hopefully, the evaluation would allow me to be a better contributor to the company.

The thing was, I never understood the need for employee evaluation. Was it supposed to make me feel more motivated to work there? Or was it supposed to make me a better accountant? If the answers were yes, then why did I feel so troubled after the meeting ended? Again, I felt like I had gone through a series of insults from a person who claimed that they were "constructive criticism".

Lynn stressed that the company used a round-table evaluation method to determine top performers and bottom performers of the company. The batch of employees who joined on the same day as me would be evaluated against each other. Then the company would give more reward to top performers and less reward to bottom performers. The top management personnel would also be seated in the meeting to facilitate the process, ensuring that the evaluation wasn't bias.

When I heard that the members of my cohort would be pitted against each other, my heart sank. Although I didn't know them as well as I knew Shan, we kept in touch quite frequently. It would definitely put a huge strain on our relationship. To be pitted against each other didn't make sense. They might as well elect me as a participant in The Hunger Games and provide me with weapons to kill my opponents. They could even say the favourite phrase in the movie, "may the odds forever be in your favour" before we slaughtered each other.

I knew that healthy competitions had made many people stronger, but nothing about that was healthy. The top performers would brag about their success while the remaining employees would feel bad about themselves. How was that healthy?

Despite the good recommendation given to me by Shan, Lynn emphasized that during her pulse check session, she discovered that I was dissatisfied with my working condition. Many things that I had mentioned during the session were brought up to evaluate my performance as an employee. I thought that the session was supposed to allow them to gain insights into my condition, so that they could help me adapt to the construction site based on my feedback. I didn't know that my feedback would be used against me. I felt like I had been stabbed in the back, and I knew exactly who stabbed me.

I also hated to be told about my weaknesses. It wasn't because I was an egomaniac who thought that I was perfect. Trust me: I have many flaws, but I didn't need to be reminded of them. I had to deal with them daily. Lynn was good with words. Instead of saying I had weaknesses, she called them "areas of improvement", but both of us knew that they were the same thing. Sugar-coating the word didn't make me feel better; it made me feel worse. Why couldn't she tell me directly without the fancy wordplay and be done with it? And why couldn't she hint to me on a monthly basis so that I could improve on my weaknesses instead of highlighting them during the employee evaluation session?

That awful session made me realize that I was seen as a coward, a person who didn't interact with others and had poor time management. I was amazed that I was all of the above, and yet I wasn't well informed about my behaviour. It was only after the employee evaluation session, I found out that I needed to make major improvements on my behaviour.

I was feeling down in the dumps, but I had to admit that Lynn was right about one thing. I had always been a coward, and I would always be one until I changed myself. I was afraid of trying new things because I feared that my life would change so drastically that I would lose everything I held dear to my heart. So, I hid behind my blanket of security, my daydreams, and my journal writings to feel safe.

I wanted to change that side of me. I must alter my destiny.

Opinions That Matter

WHEN THE NEW YEAR ARRIVED, I wasn't exactly happy. I was just glad that I had survived the employee evaluation session and the harsh condition at the construction site. I came to work one morning and saw an envelope on my desk.

I knew what was coming. Slowly, I tore open the sealed envelope, revealing my employee evaluation letter. As it turned out, my performance was merely average, and I didn't receive the promotion that I had hoped for. I felt that all my hard work had gone down the drain.

During lunch hour, I stayed in the cabin, as I was too sad to eat anything. I turned to Ping for comfort. I figured that she could help me out, even if I had to listen to her sarcastic remarks. I was really desperate.

That day, she was surprisingly quiet. She paid full attention to my rants about my career choices and my average performance as an employee.

"I've always hated the corporate world and their business performances, employee performances, and all those standard operating procedures nonsense. Performance! Performance! Performance! Come on, William, you are not a clown. You don't need to perform anything," she said after hearing my complaints. Somehow, I could sense hatred in her voice.

"Haha. You are right. Sometimes I do feel like a clown, consistently being told what to do and putting on fake smiles while people insult me. No one really knows the pain I feel inside." I forced a small laugh of frustration as I uttered those words.

I was confused about the decisions I had made in my life. Previously, I had worked as an artist who helped Ping beautify the buildings in Chinatown. Next thing I knew, I became an accountant who worked at a construction site. Now, I was treated like a clown. I was going through an identity crisis. All I wanted was to become a writer.

"Ya. No one appreciates creative people like us, William. They think that we are weirdoes. But who cares about their silly opinions and their lousy criticism, anyway? The important thing is, your parents think that you are OK. I think that you are OK. These are the opinions that matter in your life. Why don't you come back to KT? Oh. By the way, I am still a better artist compared to you." Ping seldom gave me advice, but her statement that day soothed my troubled mind, except for the better artist part.

Ping sensed my sadness and she tried her best to ease my pain, but I was still feeling sad. I didn't understand what I was sad about. Was it because I worked very hard but didn't get the promotion I wanted? Or was it because I had given up so much by coming to Kuala Lumpur? What should I do with my life?

WORST. DAY. EVER.

WHEN I ARRIVED HOME, I saw my housemate jumping up and down while screaming like a monkey that had seen something exciting for the first time.

Well, he got the promotion that he worked so hard for. He deserved to be happy.

As for me, the moment I read my employee evaluation letter, all my hopes were shattered like a plate that fell to the ground.

"Let's go out to celebrate!" He knocked loudly on my bedroom door, inviting me to go to his party, which is a very rare occasion. Although we were housemates, we seldom talked to each other. Every weekday, we were busy till midnight. Every weekend, I stayed in my room quietly while he lived the city life by partying away his worries.

"Sorry. Today is a bad day. I wasn't promoted," I replied softly. Saying those words hurt me even more.

"Still, let's go to a party. Who knows? You might get laid tonight!" He insisted happily.

"Is sex the solution to everything?" I asked, feeling annoyed.

"Well, grumpy, when was the last time you get laid?" He put a wide smile on his face, feeling confident that he was going to get lucky tonight.

"I work at the Godforsaken construction site, which is about one hour away from home. After work, I smell like crap and mud. I can't even come home on time to take a decent shower. The bricks at the construction site stand a higher chance of getting laid than me. So, my answer is … never." I let out a sigh.

"Wow. That's sad. OK. Bye!" He left the house immediately so that my negativity wouldn't ruin his magical night.

I lay in my bed, feeling exhausted. When was the last time I was *that* energetic? I used to be full of energy. At least, that was what I told myself. I was always looking for adventure and excitement when I was in Kuala Terengganu. I swam in the ocean, I hiked up the hills, and I even jogged around the park when I was free. I used to think that life in Kuala Lumpur would suit me better. It was called "the city that never sleeps" for a reason. I could attend parties and enjoy the city life to my heart's content. But it seemed that all my energy was spent at the construction site. Every night, I would come back home, drained out and ready for bed. During weekends, I wrote in my journal to temporarily escape my unbearable working life. Sometimes I wondered how Shan and the engineers survived at the construction site.

Suddenly, my daydreams were cut short when the front door burst open. I thought that that was it. That was how I was going to die, murdered by a bunch of robbers.

Instead, I heard two people laughing hysterically at each other for no good reason, accompanied by a loud limping noise which sounded like a giant with a broken leg hopping through the living room. Then, the sound of lips kissing sent an uncomfortable feeling up my spine to every end of my hair. Yes, it was so loud that I could hear it from my room!

The sound of another door slammed shut was my cue to leave the house. I wasn't ready to hear the sound of two people moaning or a bed being pushed back and forth, echoing throughout the entire house.

Wei Liem Ng

I walked to the nearest cafeteria. Actually, I ran. I ran to the nearest cafeteria. It was such a desperate scene. I thought about how unfair life was. My housemate got a promotion, and I didn't. I worked as hard as he did on every occasion.

Some people were just born lucky. Even in clubs, he could get drunk and still manage to bring a girl home with him, and it all happened within an hour! He had his promotion and was probably having sex in his room. I was forced to flee my house and run to a cafeteria all by myself in the middle of the night.

I sat alone in the corner of the cafeteria. When my food arrived, I chewed like a hungry wolf that hadn't eaten for days. I didn't care whether the food was fattening or whether it was unhealthy to eat such a heavy meal at midnight. I was ready to eat away all my hopes and dreams of ever being recognized at the company. The thought of all the crappy things that had happened to me continued to flood my mind, and tears began to overflow from my eyes.

Just when I thought that I was all alone and nobody noticed me, I overheard a conversation going on at the table beside me.

"Dude, why is that guy crying over there?"

"Man, cut him some slack, will ya? If I were as ugly as him, I would be crying too."

Worst. Day. Ever.

Decision on a Rainy Day 1

ONE BY ONE, THE RAINDROPS raced against each other, falling from the clouds and dashing quickly to the earth. I didn't realize that it had been raining for the past few minutes until I felt a tapping sensation on top of my head. When did it start to rain? In fact, why was I sitting alone on a swing in the park during a rainy day, feeling sorry for myself? When did I allow Lynn and her words to hurt me so deeply?

I had been thinking about the meeting earlier with Lynn from the human resources department. My head replayed the scene over and over again, and each time, the conversation got louder and louder. I tried to analyze her sentences. When her sentences didn't make sense, I tried to analyze her underlying meaning.

My heart was broken when I realized that I didn't receive the recognition that I had wished for. More importantly, I was devastated because I had worked very hard on the job, and despite all my efforts, I got nothing in return. When I sought an explanation from Lynn, her words hurt me even more.

With a heavy heart, I asked Lynn the reasons why I didn't get the promotion. She claimed that because I was based at the construction site, I rarely appeared at the headquarters, and my appearance was hardly noticed by the high-level managers. One of the major criteria of getting a promotion was to know how to make conversation and create good impression in front of the high-level managers. Sadly, working at the construction site diminished my opportunity to be recognized by them.

I desperately defended myself by saying that I didn't want to go to the construction site in the first place. It was said to be a challenging task, and I was convinced that it would be good for my career development, so I volunteered myself. With a serious look on her face, she told me that I decided to go there on my own accord, and if I didn't want to go to the construction site in the first place, I should've fought harder for my own benefit.

I could've sworn I had mentioned that I wasn't keen on going to the construction site, but eventually I was convinced that I was right for the job. I ended up working there because she convinced me to do so, but now she was highlighting that it was my own decision.

I felt like the naive kid in school who was cheated by the bully to give away his lunch money. When the bully was caught red handed by the teacher, the naive kid was forced to say that he donated the money willingly to help the bully.

Hurt by her words, I felt the need to defend myself further. I mentioned that I had stayed late after work every day to finish up the administrative work. Unlike the headquarters, the construction site didn't have the luxury of an admin department, and all administrative work was nonchalantly passed to the finance department. It was a burdensome task, often repetitive, and it required my effort to negotiate with different parties on a daily basis, but I did it anyway. I was willing to do it. I took up those tasks because she had told me that it would be good for my career development. I wanted to climb the corporate ladder to be as successful as the CEO one day. I had abandoned my hometown in search of better opportunities. I needed to know that there was still hope for me at the company.

With a collected posture and a stern face, Lynn insisted that my actions were unproductive. No matter how much administrative work that I decided to do, in the end, it wouldn't result in paving a pathway to a good career. It would *never* help me grow as an accountant, nor would it make me a better CEO. CEOs didn't spend their time doing administrative work; they leveraged it on other people.

I was dumbfounded. What she said had a hint of truth in it, but it hit me where it hurt most. I felt like I had climbed a ladder made of sharp blades just to reach the top. When I was finally at the top, I was greeted by a thousand knives that pieced through my heart.

Crying in front of her would show a sign of weakness, but I couldn't sit in the same room with her any longer. I politely excused myself and ended the meeting. I bottled up my emotions as I walked out of the human resources department with my head held high, away from Lynn and away from the people in the department who claimed that they stood up for every employee's best interest. I didn't know how I did it, but I managed to get through the day without shedding a single tear.

That evening, as I sat on the swing, where everyone I knew was out of sight, I rocked myself back and forth while tears streamed down my cheeks and blended themselves with the raindrops. I couldn't hold it in any longer. I wasn't strong enough to handle so much criticism in a day. My sadness was overwhelming my fragile mind. So I cried and cried under the pouring rain.

Perhaps Lynn was right after all. Perhaps I brought this upon myself. Perhaps every single thing was done based on my own decision. On that rainy day, I decided to cry alone on a swing.

A Stroll to Heal the Soul

I T RAINED CONTINUOUSLY FOR TWO days, and I was unable to do anything to distract my mind. So I stayed in my room the entire weekend. It was such a bad idea. Every song that I listened to reminded me of my broken dream. I turned to my pints of ice cream to eat away my feelings, but it didn't work. Everything reminded me of that awful feeling of being hurt by Lynn's words. I wasted my weekend bathing myself in tears, crying and crying until my eyes were swollen.

When Monday finally arrived, I realized that I couldn't go to work, not like that. I could hardly focus on anything, let alone the complex figures on the Excel sheets. I would just be counting the hours till it was time for me to leave work. More importantly, I didn't want Shan to know about my sadness. Her work was tough enough; it would be unfair for her to console me about my problems too.

I made a phone call to Shan, pleading to take a day off to organize my thoughts. Her voice was very comforting. She allowed me to rest and take good care of myself. She knew that I was upset. Sometimes, I felt that she knew exactly how I felt about a certain tragedy because she would come to my aid by saying the right things at the right time to lessen my sorrow.

After I hung up the phone, I slowly drove myself to the nearest park. The sun was rising slowly that day, working its way to the top of the sky and chasing away the mist that blanketed the surface of the earth. The rain for the past two days had managed to balance the temperature well. The weather was just nice, not too warm and not too cold.

I took a long stroll around the park, circling the jogging tracks as I breathed in the morning air. It was very refreshing. I could feel that the air was clear, unlike the dust-filled air at the construction site, which carried a rotten smell.

While walking, I gazed upon the tall green trees that surrounded the park. I felt like I had been teleported away from the hustle and bustle of the city into a magnificent painting.

Beautiful scenery always gave me a sense of peace and tranquillity. I felt like I was in Kuala Terengganu again. My soul was slowly healing; the pain I had felt a few days ago faded away into nature.

Trees had a way of absorbing sadness. They transferred my sorrow into their leaves. As the leaves waxed and waned with time, so did my sadness.

Unlike the depressing music that I listened to all weekend, the sound of birds chirping, accompanied by rustling leaves as silhouettes in the background, was very uplifting. It had been a long time since I had heard birds singing their melodious tune and I really appreciated them for singing their hearts out every morning.

Slowly, my thoughts started to unclutter, and my restoration process began. Though I was far from being happy, at least I wasn't sad anymore. It was like a plaster had been placed upon the wound on my heart and the bleeding stopped. Taking a day off to stroll in the park was exactly what I needed to rejuvenate my body and my mind.

When I was tired of walking, I sat alone in the park, eyeing the leaves as they detached themselves from the branches and floated along with the breeze that carried them gently to the ground. For the first time in a very long while, I was untroubled by noisy machines and incoming e-mails. I remembered what it was like to be carefree again, even though it was just for a day.

Delaying
My Zombification Process

I ARRIVED TO WORK EARLY THE next day after taking a day off and bought myself a cup of hot chocolate from Starbucks. Although the drink was severely overpriced, I needed it. I heard that chocolate helps the body to release serotonin and dopamine, the "feel good" hormones, and I desperately wanted the hot chocolate to make me feel happy again.

I had been staring at my drink for a while now, imagining that after the magical drink entered my body, my happiness would somehow return to me.

I cupped the bottom of the oversized cup firmly, spinning the cup in a clockwise motion with just enough force to let the hot chocolate hit the sides of the cup. I smiled softly as I watched the hot chocolate try to escape my cup like a rough brown sea during a thunderstorm. The waves crashed against the tall rocks, desperately trying to reach the other side.

"What are you doing smiling at your drink like that?" Shan said as though it was the weirdest thing she had seen all morning. My fantasy world crumbled before my eyes. The rough brown sea came to a halt.

"Nothing. Nothing really," I replied as I fixed my gaze on her face, forcing an awkward smile to ease the situation. I wasn't fully myself yet.

The wrinkles on her forehead slowly faded away. Then, she told me that the universe had decided to punish her by creating a massive traffic jam just before she left her house. Every driver in front of her was a bad driver, and their sole purpose was to test her patience. Being an impatient driver all her life, she told me that she passed her patience test with flying colours that day, because she didn't honk at anyone, not even once. She just sat in her car and cussed at all of them. If they couldn't hear it, it didn't count.

I laughed at her painful morning experience. In the meantime, I tried to recall the last time I got stuck in traffic. I couldn't remember any details about my morning routine besides the day I had to lie about my "illness". My mind was blank every single morning when I travelled to work. It was then and there that I realized I had an autopilot mode.

When I did something so frequently in my daily life, my mind automatically shut down. I knew exactly what I was doing, but I wasn't thinking about anything. It was as though my brain malfunctioned due to my repetitive actions.

I woke up to my alarm at five thirty every morning. Then, I would groggily turn off the alarm because I knew that there would be another alarm at five forty. I wondered why I bothered to set the five thirty alarm in the first place. I had always wanted to wake up at five thirty to get a ten-minute head start, but my laziness would get the better of me.

Next, I would drag myself into the kitchen, pour myself a glass of warm water, and drink it while I was still half asleep until the first stream of hot water caressed my face in the shower. While my eyes were still struggling to stay open, I put on my ever so boring brown work uniform and rolled my eyes in disgust as I remembered that my friend Ping hated the colour brown. She claimed that my life was exactly like crap because I dressed in brown attire most of the time.

Eventually, I would take the crowded train at six fifteen to the construction site. The train would be filled with working adults in their formal attire, looking down on their smartphones, reading their morning paper, or taking a short nap. There would be huge frowns on their faces, as though they dreaded waking up so early but had to do it anyway. Then, I would space out for an hour. When I finally reached the construction site, I would take another five-minute walk into my work cabin and start filling in figures on Excel sheets.

My greatest fear was materializing before my eyes. I was becoming a working zombie like most of the adults in Kuala Lumpur. Life would be meaningless. The only motivation to keep me going was money, money, and more money.

I needed to delay my zombification process before it was too late. I refused to become like the secretary I met before my interview, with her acrylic nails hitting the keyboard as she stared at her computer screen, ignoring the world around her. I needed to keep my mind alive. I wanted to be creative again.

A *Boring* Day at Work

S HAN CAME BACK INTO THE cabin drenched in sweat. While she
took off her safety equipment, she had a soft smile plastered on
her face. She looked at me; her smile widened even more, with words
almost spilling out of her mouth.

"What's up with you?" I asked, feeling curious about her sudden
happiness. Sometimes, I wished I could be as bubbly as her.

"Nothing. I just inspected the engineers as they did their *boring*
job. See what I did there? I made a pun." She laughed at herself,
feeling triumphant that she had come up with a pun after walking
around the construction site.

Considering the boring work conducted by boring machines,
boring tools, and boring accessories, it was about time someone came
up with a pun. Boring had officially become the most commonly
used word at the construction site.

Jokes aside, I was bored with my work, handling administrative
issues and looking at Excel sheets day in and day out without
undertaking interesting tasks. What if that was it? What if there were
no interesting tasks? Was I going to balance figures on Excel sheets
at the construction site for the next forty years until I retired, old and
unable to work any longer? That wasn't how I imagined my life to be.

When a person is bored with his daily job, he seeks comfort in
the arms of his friends. In my case, I voiced my concerns to my boss.

When I said "voiced my concerns", I meant that I was complaining about how boring my job was and saying that if I were to do the same thing any longer, I would go mad, bury my laptop at the construction site, and pour concrete over it.

Shan listened attentively to my words, occasionally nodding in agreement. She had the ability to shut out the entire world, even the annoying background noise made by the machines, and focus all her attention and care towards my problems. She remained silent throughout my rants, and in that silence, I believed that she understood me. After a short while, she smiled at me again. The same victorious expression was on her face when she had made the pun earlier. "Why don't you say so? I am happy to give some of my work to you. I will get back to you tomorrow, I promise!" She gave me a thumbs-up and ended the discussion merrily.

The discussion was short, but somehow a lot had been accomplished in that brief moment. I could sense that my problems would magically disappear after talking to her. Shan was a clear example of a great leader. She listened and took action to help her subordinate.

An Interesting Meeting

S HAN WAS THE TYPE OF person who kept her word. She promised me that she would give me an interesting task. On the next day, she delivered on her promise. As she stood in front of me, she faked a cough to capture my attention.

"Ahem. William, would you like to accompany me to the meeting with subcontractors tomorrow? They are going to paint murals on our barricade around the construction site," Shan said while stretching out her arm and handing me a piece of paper filled with colour palette.

"Finally! Something interesting to do around here. I thought I was going to die of boredom." I snatched the paper from her hand and smiled.

"Dramatic as usual, William." She shook her head. We both laughed at my actions.

It had been a while since something interesting happened at the construction site. Recently, there wasn't much progress aside from the gradual increase in piling work. A weekly report was pasted beside the entrance of the cabin to motivate all of us. The previous report stated "218 piles completed! 42 more to go!" and when the next week arrived, the new report stated "220 piles completed! 40 more to go!" Every week, the same sentences were used, the same exclamation points were placed at the exact location, and the same Arial Black font was used. Only the numbers changed. The report wasn't designed to motivate employees; it was designed make everyone more depressed than ever.

It came to my realization that I was upset with many things at the construction site. Perhaps not everything was boring at the site; I was just bored with everything. When there was a meeting about painting the barricade surrounding the construction site, I was happy that Shan invited me. I wanted the construction site to have life. I wanted the wonderful feeling of admiring the murals along the barricade before entering my cabin every day.

Before the meeting began, I was already on cloud nine, dreaming about meeting interesting people who shared the same passion as my friend Ping, people who talked about the work of art they created and how they breathed life into their work.

I couldn't wait for the next day. It would be the most interesting meeting since I had started working at the site.

Watching Paint Dry

S HAN AND I WERE IN the meeting room, waiting patiently for the subcontractors from a paint company to arrive. While she was scrolling through her messages on her smartphone, I fixed my gaze upon the door of the meeting room like a little puppy waiting for its owner to arrive home. I looked at my laptop screen. It was five minutes to nine o'clock. They would arrive any time soon.

My heart was filled with glee as I imagined the grey barricade that surrounded the construction site going through a drastic transformation. The barricade would be our empty canvas, decorated by a splendid burst of blue, green, yellow, and orange. The wonderful murals would be the fruit of our imagination.

I was an inexperienced painter, but I managed to learn a few things when I helped Ping paint her murals on the buildings in Kuala Terengganu. She taught me that bright colours could have a positive effect on a person's mood.

Most people spent their days in black, blue, and white, feeling down about themselves, which was why bright colours such as yellow, orange, and red would capture their attention and lighten their mood. When people witnessed bright colours, it gave them a sense of warmth and a feeling of excitement. While it was important to include bright colours in murals, a painter must strike a balance, using cool colours such as blue and green to give the crowd a sense of thrill and tranquillity at the same time.

My mind wandered off into the future. We would paint a grassy field on the grey barricade, stretching as far as one's eye could see. There were herds of cows and sheep slowly munching away their worries in the background. There were flowers presenting their beautiful colours for the world to see, and children were playing joyfully with their friends. On top of that, a clear blue sky was looking down upon them, with little clouds in sight. The murals on the barricade would be the centre of attention in the dull city.

Suddenly, the door of the meeting room swung open, two formally dressed people walked into the room, each carrying a briefcase. As they sat in front of Shan and me, we started our discussion. They took out their palette and showed us the colour of their choice: green.

Green? Just green? No one could paint a masterpiece with just one colour. It was impossible. I had thought that we were going to discuss the works of art which we would paint on the barricade. As it turned out, I was supposed to discuss with the subcontractors which type of green would be most suitable on a grey barricade. I was given a choice between apple green, olive green, lime green, and other shades of green that I didn't understand. They dipped a paintbrush into one of the green paints and drew a stroke on a piece of paper, watched in amazement as the paint dried, and explained to me the quality of their paint.

After all that hype and all that wonderful imagination, I was greeted by two people who were excited about which type of green I would choose and hopefully sign a contract with them. I could see that the field of joy and happiness faded into darkness. Immediately, my dream was crumpled and thrown into a rubbish bin, and no one could understand my pain. I should've known not to trust artists who dressed in formal attire. They weren't artists; they were merely paint salesmen.

In the end, I chose dark green. I was disappointed. My mood was dark, so dark green was the perfect choice. For the remainder of the meeting, we discussed the quantity of paint needed and the rate per hour that we needed to pay the workers for painting the barricade. The meeting went on for an hour, and I was struggling to keep my eyes open.

The meeting with those subcontractors drained every ounce of my energy. It was exactly like watching paint dry, literally.

The Manager Who Died

I T WAS WAY PAST MY working hours, and yet I was still sitting in the cabin with Shan, working on our presentation slides for an important meeting the next day. I whined about how sick and tired I was of the construction site. Nothing interesting ever happened there. Then, she told me a scary story about the manager who died at the construction site.

A few months before I joined the company, a manager died in the middle of the night while he was working. Many stories were told about the manager's death. Some said that he overworked himself to death. He often pulled an all-nighter. One morning, out of the blue, he was found cold on his desk by the workers. Others who were more creative said that the construction site was haunted, and vengeful spirits had been draining his life force every night; finally, his life force was depleted, and he passed out stone cold on his desk. The stories told about that man had one similarity: he worked until midnight, just like the two of us at that moment.

An e-mail was sent by the top management team to all the staff upon his death. It stated that he was a hard-working man. The company was deeply burdened by the loss of a diligent and dedicated employee who gave an unremitting struggle to perform his best and sacrifice everything for the company. May he rest in peace. The e-mail was beautifully written, thanks to the branding and marketing department, but after I read the e-mail, instead of feeling sorry for him, I got an entirely different vibe.

All I understood from the e-mail was, "Hello lads, new rules over here. See the man who set a shining example? Working yourself to death *is* now the minimum requirement for a promotion."

Our colleagues at the headquarters often sent us e-mails stressing the importance of having work-life balance, but none of them bothered to experience the scenarios we faced at the construction site. If only they could understand the pain that we went through, dealing with an unfavourable environment and taking on sudden challenges while trying desperately to breathe in clean air, they would've been more considerate towards our struggles instead of preaching to us from their high horses.

The thought of the manager who passed away haunted me deeply. Was I destined to work myself to death and let people write eulogies about my great sacrifice?

There seemed to be no future for me there. I stayed on because I thought that I wanted to become a better accountant, but it was clear to me that I was going nowhere.

Moving Forward

The Turning Point

I FELT LIKE I WAS TRAVELLING along the journey of life with no end in sight. I was just driving and driving, without a clear destination. I wondered when I would see a junction or a sign that read taking that road was a mistake to begin with, and I should immediately make a big U-turn.

I believed that in everybody's life, there would be a turning point. Something drastic would happen to that person and give him a wake-up call. Then, he would have to decide which course of action he should take in order to find himself again.

For my friend Yap, his turning point was when he served as a volunteer in Africa, providing healthcare for the less fortunate. He realized the importance of contributing to society, and he wanted to do that for a living. Since he was already majoring in dentistry, his experience in Africa solidified his dream of becoming a better dentist. Now, he served as a dentist to provide top-notch oral care to all of his patients.

For my friend Ping, her turning point was when she built her own company. As a freelance artist, she was afraid of commitment. She didn't want to burden herself with the responsibilities of being a boss. When she was finally brave enough to form her own company, she was dedicated to making it the most creative company possible that gave joy to all the locals in Kuala Terengganu.

If there were three levels of feeling down about myself, they would be rock bottom, the void of nothingness, and, one level lower, my current condition. I decided to seek advice from Shan. I needed to know that I was worth something to the company. I finally understood the reason why engineers sought comfort and advice from Shan. It was because she truly cared about the well-being of others.

Throughout our conversation, she was very sincere and objective, not as a boss towards her subordinate but as a friend who cared deeply about my direction in life. She told me that it was important to chase my own dream if my job was making me unhappy. She said, "Life is too short to waste a minute of it doing a job you don't like or care about. If you weren't doing your current job today, would you apply for it? Would you get it?"

Yes, life is too short indeed. I should do the things I loved, and that was definitely not working as an accountant at a construction site. I was getting used to the harsh environment, and I was blending in with the engineers, but my job wasn't making me happy. In fact, I hadn't felt happy about myself for quite a long time. I had forgotten what it felt like to have joy in my daily life. Balancing figures on an Excel sheet didn't make me happy. Writing did, always had, and always would.

It was time for me to move on with my life. No one was in charge of my happiness – not my friends, not my job, and certainly not the salary that the company paid me. But, I was afraid of what might happen if I decided to chase my dream. What if I made the U-turn but there was nothing there to begin with?

I felt like I was at a crossroad again. I had returned to the time when I finished my ACCA exams. I was left with two choices: to continue as an accountant or to give up everything and become a writer.

How Much Time
Do I Have Left?

T HE PHONE CALL FROM PING an hour ago had kept me awake on
my bed. Besides the usual sarcasm towards my career choice,
she told me that she had taken up a lot of projects for her business.
She felt overwhelmed but excited at the same time. She bragged
about her artistic nature, her one-of-a-kind negotiation skills, and
how the two came together to land her many new projects for her
company. She stressed that her time was precious and she felt like
she wasn't doing enough to grow her business. When I asked her
to elaborate her reasons for taking up so many projects, instead of
giving me a direct answer like everyone else, she told me a story
about mankind.

Once upon a time in heaven, God summoned a dog, a cow, and
a human. First, God said to the dog, "You are to stay at home and
look after the house. In return, I shall grant you a life span of three
decades."

The dog wasn't greedy. It said, "I only need one decade."

"Deal!" God said, and the dog was sent to earth.

Next, God faced the cow and said, "You are to work very hard
and serve others. In return, I shall grant you a life span of five
decades."

The cow was also not greedy. It said, "I only need two decades."

"I will accept that," God said, and the cow was sent to earth.

Lastly, God said to the human, "You are to enjoy life, but I shall grant you a life span of only two decades."

The human was deeply unsatisfied. Filled with greed, the human said, "God, you have two decades from the dog and three decades from the cow. Can you add their life span to mine?" Reluctantly, God agreed to the human's request. That was how a human's life span came to be.

An average human spends two decades having the time of his life, three decades working like a cow to earn money, and two final decades staying at home, looking after his house like a dog.

I was pretty sure that the moral of the story was you need to be content with what you had, but Ping saw a different lesson. She pointed out that humans have an average life span of seven decades. Two decades had passed, and she hadn't accomplished anything significant in her life. She wanted to spend the remaining five decades making her mark on the world. She advised me to think clearly about the ways to spend my remaining five decades and promptly hung up the phone.

I remembered vividly when I started writing my first word on my ACCA exam paper. Every five to ten minutes, I would raise my head to look at the huge clock hanging on the wall to see how much time I had left. At that moment, time seemed to be the most important thing. Every second and minute that passed was a countdown towards the end of my ACCA exam. In life, I had never bothered to measure the time I had left until I would be lying down stone cold inside my coffin. I had always taken time for granted because I assumed that I would have more the next day. There was always a tomorrow. But that night, Ping's advice hit an uncomfortable place in my heart. Two decades of my life had just come and gone. I would be considered lucky if I had five more decades, but what if I didn't?

Ten years is a lot of time. Many things could happen in ten years. Similarly, nothing could happen in ten years if I did nothing.

I would like to have a lot of money. Who wouldn't? But if I spent ten years of my life working up the corporate ladder, would I be satisfied at the end of it, or would I be miserable like the engineers at the construction site, complaining about their job? I only have one life, and ten years *is* a lot of time. I might as well do something about the time I had left to live my life to the fullest.

Thoughts about my future started to drown my mind. As much as I tossed and turned in my bed, I couldn't sleep. Within a few hours, I needed to wake up, shower, and go to work. At work, I would be burdened with more ideas and more problems, which would prevent me from thinking about the things I truly wanted. I needed to do something about my life so that I wouldn't live to regret my future.

Be Fully Prepared

I WAS CAUGHT IN BETWEEN GIVING my notice of resignation and continuing my career as an accountant. If I chose the first option, I could be living my dream as a poor adult. If I chose to stay, I would be rich but miserable. I couldn't decide which was worse. Sometimes, I hoped that the hardest decision in life would be automatically decided for me.

Thankfully, Yap was on his vacation in Kuala Lumpur. I invited him over to my house to have a chat, desperately hoping that he could shed some light upon my shadowy future.

"Can I put my hand in your mouth?" Yap blurted out suddenly while we were in the midst of discussing my life options.

"What? Ew! No! That's disgusting!" I was confused.

"What if I put my gloves on?" He took out a pair of plastic gloves from his wallet. Seriously, I knew that he was a dentist, but who would keep rubber gloves in his wallet?

"What the heck? No!" I shook my head wildly.

"What if I give you ten *Ringgit*?" He took out a ten-*Ringgit* note and stretched it in front of my face. He then put it on the table and continued to pull out a dental explorer and a mouth mirror from his pocket.

"One hundred *Ringgit*!" I exclaimed. What was I thinking?

"Deal! A verbal agreement is considered an oral contract and is legally binding." He smiled. At the same time, he put on his gloves and let go of the rubber as it snapped against his wrist.

I knew I was screwed. I couldn't make informed decisions under pressure. Besides, how could I say no to one hundred *Ringgit*? More importantly, how could I say no to Yap? He was fully prepared to give me a dental check-up.

After checking my teeth, he advised me to go for a scaling session at the nearest dental clinic and then, I would be as good as new. Once again, I ended up not taking his money.

Aside from having to take extra good care of my oral hygiene, I learnt something from Yap that day. When he set his mind to do something, he was fully prepared to go for it. I too, should prepare myself if I wanted to chase my dream.

Detachment

I WAS STILL EXTREMELY DISSATISFIED THAT day. When I invited Yap over to my house, I wasn't asking for a dental check-up. I was going to ask him whether I should just give my resignation letter and be done with it, and I was hoping that he would decide for me. After pacing in circles around the sofa in my living room, I decided to call Yap to hear his opinions about my life crisis.

If you call a friend during midnight and he is willing to answer, you know that you have a great friend. Picking up the phone is already a plus point, and if he is willing to squeeze his brain juice to give you advice, there is no doubt in the world that he is indeed a true friend.

Yap picked up my call, groggily said that he would call me in five minutes, and immediately hung up. Exactly five minutes later, my phone rang, and I answered it. Yap was back to his usual self, full of energy and life, ready to take on my questions. It was as though in that five minutes, he had transformed into another person.

"Hi, William. So, you were saying?" he greeted me with excitement.

"I wanted to know whether I should hang on to my job or leave it." I went straight to the point, fearing that he would stray away from the topic like our previous chat.

"Actually, what are you hanging on to? Your job? Wealth? Position? Or fame? In the process of chasing those elements, you are enslaved by them. I haven't seen you feeling happy for a while now. Hanging on to those things is much more painful than letting them go. You should learn about detachment." He gave me his philosophical speech, enunciating each sentence clearly so that I could grasp what he meant.

I laughed hysterically as I pointed out that his mental wires must have short-circuited due to his endless dental consultations. How could anyone be truly detached from those elements? Owning nothing in life would be horrible! I would be exactly like the homeless on the streets, begging people for money to get through the day. My life would be in chaos! I told him that there was no way in hell I would beg for anything!

"Detachment is not that you own nothing, is that nothing should own you." He said the sentence softly and slowly through the phone, like a lecturer educating his confused student.

The whole conversation was a blur. He was very wise with his vocabulary and philosophies. Apparently, he was more enlightened after a good sleep. After a short while, I started to feel bad about interrupting his sleep, so I quickly ended the phone call. I did have a tiny bit of courtesy left in me.

I reflected on our conversation after the phone call. I wasn't clinging on to wealth, position, or fame. None of those mattered to me. I was clinging on to security. Although my life was difficult, I was getting accustomed to it. Getting out of my comfort zone would mean that I needed to adapt to a new environment all over again. I didn't fully understand what he meant by practicing detachment, but I did understand one thing: nothing should own me. I mustn't let anyone or anything get in my way of achieving my dream.

Decision on a Rainy Day 2

I T WAS ONE OF THOSE days when everything didn't go according to plan. Everything in the universe suddenly decided to join forces just to make my life miserable, and it all began with the traffic congestion happening outside my cabin.

Despite the sound of heavy machines drilling into the ground, the noise of people cursing like it was the end of the world and cars honking furiously at each other still managed to reach my ears, pounding loudly against my eardrums. It was then that I decided I would stay back and get some work done. Besides, the hours spent being squeezed inside the train with the crowd were better spent doing my work anyway.

It was only at 10:00 p.m. that the traffic started to ease. Thinking that it was a good sign, I packed my belongings and dashed towards the front door, already thinking about resting in my cosy bed. Suddenly, the zinc roof of the cabin made that familiar tapping sound I hated. It had begun to rain. I stared at the light drizzle, thinking that if I made a dash for it, I could still make it to the train station. Before I could finish planning my escape from the construction site, the drizzle quickly became a heavy shower. Within minutes, the heavy shower evolved into a torrential downpour.

I was determined to get home, so I searched my cabin high and low for an umbrella, a sign that good luck was still on my side and

I could finally go home. Instead of finding my umbrella, I found a note saying, "William, I took ur umbrella bcoz it looks like it's gonna rain. TQ!". Someone borrowed my umbrella because it looked like it was going to rain? Why couldn't they leave my umbrella behind because I was actually stuck with the rain?

I was trapped in my cabin, unable to go anywhere because someone had robbed me of my opportunity to go home without getting soaked by the rain. When all hope seemed lost, I sighed and sank into my office chair, thinking of my colleagues at the headquarters. They were probably smiling with happiness even though it was pouring because the building had an underground car park. I could be driving home right now if I were at the headquarters, but as Lynn pointed out, I had willingly decided to be based at the construction site. Maybe she was right after all. I had decided to take up the challenge of working at the construction site. I had decided not to get promoted because the top management personnel didn't even know that I existed. I had decided to work late and got myself trapped in this predicament. I had decided to accept my fate without doing anything about it.

"Today is not the day that I decide to cry in the rain. To hell with the human resources department, the top management team, and the rain that prevent me from going to the train station. Today is the day I take charge of my own destiny. I decide *when* my life is miserable." I told myself, beaming with confidence.

I slammed my hands against my desk and stood up straight, more confident than ever before. As I locked the cabin door behind me, I took a deep breath and dashed through the torrential rain, trying my best to maintain my balance as I ran through the uneven ground. I felt mud splashing on my pants as I occasionally stepped into a pothole. My body got heavier by the minute as my shirt and pants soaked up the mud and rainwater. Eventually, mud had entered my shoes and my feet weighed like a ton, but I journeyed on. With each step I took, I was closer and closer to the train station.

When I reached the entrance of the station, I dashed inside and burst out laughing at myself because I was soaking wet from head to toe. I didn't care about the glaring stares from the people around me. They probably thought that I was a maniac, but I was so happy that I had run through the pouring rain. For the first time in a very long time, I took control of my own destiny.

Two Steps Forward, One Step Back

S TANDING IN FRONT OF THE human resources department at nine in the morning when everyone was about to start work wasn't how I pictured my day at the headquarters. Every colleague who passed by me paused for few seconds, smiled at me, and quickly went inside the office to sit at their cubicle. I disliked their smile, I hated everyone in that department, and most of all, I dreaded myself for being in front of that department. I knew that it was unfair to judge my other colleagues in the same department just because I had a manipulative supervisor, but I was hurt. I hastily assumed that everyone who worked in that department was as awful as her. The engineers at site told me that human resources personnel only cared about the well-being of the company, not my personal well-being. Stereotypes were there for a reason. I wanted to believe what they said. No, I must believe what they said in order to do what was right for me.

With the resignation letter in my hand, I paced towards the front entrance of the office. As if the door were a powerful barrier, I paused and turned back to face the lift that I had come out of, moving two steps forward and then one step back. I couldn't bring myself to walk through that door.

What if I continued working for the company? What would happen to me? I wanted to believe that I had opportunities there, that I was recognized as a talented employee, and that I would have a bright future at the company. A few years down the road, I would be a great team leader who coaches his employees to be productive at work. But those were merely false hopes. None of them were true. I would have to work for another year to prove that I was worthy of a promotion. All of that for what? To bring me a step closer to my dream? I wanted to be a writer, not an accountant.

On the other hand, what if I gave my notice of resignation? Would everything change for the better? I wanted to write my own book. I wanted to share my story with the world, but would that bring food to the table? I don't wish to be the son who depends on his parents for the rest of his life.

To dream was one thing, to make it a reality was another.

Deep down, I knew I was scared. I was scared to face the changes after I resigned. Staying wasn't an option. My future wasn't with the company. No matter how scared I was, I must move forward.

"No! No more turning back! I need to do this. I *must*." I uttered those words out loud so that I could hear them myself. Everything in my mind began to make sense. Those words were like magic. They uncluttered my thoughts and realigned them into a sequence. I knew what I had to do. I walked through the door of no return.

People Change

I WAS SITTING QUIETLY IN MY little room, trying to understand how I had summoned the courage to submit my resignation letter. "Great!" My mind yelled the word in my head while I forcefully faked a wide smile on my face. Two months from now, I would be a jobless adult without a clear future.

There was one friend who would surely find my news interesting. I picked up my phone and dialled Ping's number to tell her about my decision that morning. I didn't care that it was already 1:00 a.m.; news that was as great as mine had to be shared.

Two seconds later, she answered my call. I assumed that she must be busy working on one of her projects because she would normally be asleep at that hour.

"Hi, William. So you quit your job?" was her first sentence when I greeted her. It had been a year since she tirelessly persuaded me to leave my job and chase my own dream.

"Yes, Ping, I quit." I emphasized every word of my sentence clearly.

"You are bullshitting, right? I mean ..." she said in confusion.

"No! Really, I quit." I interrupted her.

"Oh my goodness! Are you freaking serious? Wow! You got your balls back! Oh! Oh! You can fly back to KT. Heck, I will even buy you your flight tickets. You can help me with my projects to boost your

123

creative juice. You can finally write your book, something that you wanted to do for a long time. You can travel to see the world. You can do so many things! I am so excited for you." She was screaming on the phone, and I could hear her excitement emanating through her voice at the other end of the line. There was so much positivity in her voice. It was as though I had achieved my dream and she was celebrating with me.

We had a very long and interesting conversation. She told me that brown was still her most hated colour in the whole wide world but she had come to terms with the colour beige. Apparently, although beige has a hint of basic brown, the majority of it is white. She joked about how a zombie could transform back into a normal human being if he were given the right antidote and promptly related the joke to my current condition. I wasn't offended at all. Both of us had a good laugh about me. I confessed to her that I really wanted to go back to Kuala Terengganu, back to the quiet town where there was complete silence at night, and back to my home where everything was warm and cosy. I could get used to a life away from the busy city.

I thought that I could search for opportunities while I worked in Kuala Lumpur. As it turned out, I was wrong. I was so occupied with work that I hardly allowed myself some free time to search for the things I came here for in the first place. Besides, it didn't matter where the place was; opportunities were everywhere. I just needed to muster enough courage to grab them myself.

As much as I wanted to chat until the sun rose, I needed my sleep. I had to go to work the next day and start my countdown until I left the company. Hence, I ended our phone call abruptly. She was very supportive towards my decision. Surprisingly, not many insults were launched throughout our conversation. She gave me many good insights about writing my book, about finding inspiration through my daily activities, and about persevering towards my dream although it might seem impossible.

People once said that a leopard can never change its spots. Obviously, they hadn't meet Ping, because I felt that she had transformed into a different person that day. I had never seen Ping being supportive towards my decisions before, but I witnessed a miracle that day. To be more precise, I heard it with my own ears. She was genuinely happy for me.

Tired of Fighting

As I was browsing through my inbox, I saw an e-mail with the title "Exit Interview" sent by Shan. After I gave my notice of resignation, there were only two types of e-mails that appeared frequently in my mailbox. Number one was to organize a farewell lunch or dinner party to officially send me away. Number two was to meet with bosses and colleagues to explain my reasons for leaving the company. Shan's e-mail was the latter.

Seeing that it was an important issue, she wanted to speak with me privately. As I knocked on the meeting room door, I suddenly felt a lump forming in my throat. I attempted desperately to swallow it, but it seemed to have a way of clinging on to my throat. I knew that I was nervous about everything that happened: attending the meeting, leaving the company, and most of all, talking to the one person who understood me the most.

Shan had a way of asking the right questions, the questions that mattered to me deep inside. There was a moment of silence when we both looked at each other in the meeting room. Then, she smiled softly to ease the tension.

"William, am I a bad leader?" she asked weakly, unlike her usual active self. My thoughts were racing and spinning out of control. I didn't understand why she asked the question. I didn't know how to answer either.

"It's OK, William. You can be honest, since you are about to leave the company already." She smiled at me again.

"No. It's not you. It's just that … I'm just … tired," I answered her question as my lips trembled and my mind struggled to construct a proper sentence. There was a long pause. Confusion was written across her face.

"Tired? Like how?" She asked again, raising her eyebrows. Every time she asked a question, she had the element of sincerity. Her heart was in the right place. It wasn't about the company. It was *never* about the company. She cared deeply for all her colleagues at the construction site, including me. She made me feel safe enough to voice out my true feelings without being manipulated. Just like that, my world's best-kept secret flowed out of my mouth.

My tears streamed down my cheeks as I told her about my awful experience. It wasn't her that made me want to leave the company. I had been naive enough to believe that there was a chance for me to grow there. I thought that I wanted to become a successful accountant, but all I wanted was to become a writer. I was tired, tired of fighting everything and everyone around me. It seemed like every battle in which I came out victorious was always short-lived. There was always another battle around the corner, and the war could never be won. I was tired of fighting to pass my ACCA exams. I was tired of going for interviews, tired of competing against thousands of graduates who tried to take my position at the company. I fought for survival in the harsh environment, for the promotion that I didn't get because I was at the construction site instead of staying at the headquarters. I fought against my inner self every day to go to work as an accountant when I should've just chased my dream like everyone else. I was always fighting. And at that moment, I was fighting my tears, which had decided to welcome themselves upon my cheeks uninvited. I felt drained, and I couldn't continue any longer.

I needed to break free from my insecurities, the chains that bound me to the corporate world. I must chase my dream. I didn't wish to be old one day, working at my job while regretting my life decisions. Even if I failed in the process of chasing my dream, I would be content. At least I had given it my all. I had to move on with my life.

A Happy Ending?

D URING MY FINAL DAY AT the construction site, as I packed my stuff into a box, I looked at my calendar for the last time. There were still plenty of meetings to attend and many more e-mails to send, but I was no longer obligated to do any of those things. The company would carry on as usual. My absence wouldn't impact the company's operation in any way. I was merely a low-ranking executive at a company that had been well established throughout Malaysia for more than forty years. How could I have any significant impact on it? I wished to say that I had contributed a little bit. At least I had grown strong enough to be able to walk freely at the construction site, and I had helped Shan to balance her monthly financial statements. But all those things didn't matter anymore, because I was leaving her. I was leaving the company for good.

Most journeys had a positive outcome, and most stories had a happy ending. I wouldn't call leaving the company a happy ending, at least not for Shan. She had started working at the construction site as a single accountant, handling all the admin-related matters while trying her best to prepare monthly financial statements for the top management team so that they could urge the engineers to increase their productivity. Eventually, the engineers would gather at the corner of her room to rant about their problems while seeking consolation from her. She had to juggle all those things on a daily basis, which caused her to work late into the night.

When I became her assistant, for a brief moment I did help her relieve some of her burden. After I abandoned her, she would be in the same situation like when she first started working at the construction site. Would I say that her situation was a happy ending? Absolutely not.

As for me, I no longer had to take further criticism from Lynn, which was generally a good outcome. At the same time, I felt like I was leaving so much behind. I wouldn't be able to listen to the funny stories from the engineers who often worked late at night. I was leaving behind the opportunity to learn many wonderful lessons from a great boss.

"I am leaving my career as an accountant behind, for what? To chase my dream as a writer? I am acting like a total lunatic. My actions are crazy, and they scare the living daylights out of me. There is no perfect sunset and there is no shining castle. There is not even a beautiful princess waiting to be rescued. I am venturing into a future with absolutely no certainty, and I am alone on this journey." Thoughts about my future started pouring into my head.

"Hello, hello? Earth to William." Shan waved a marker pen rapidly back and forth in front of my face. The marker pen was swaying so fast, each of its movements was like a spinning blade, cutting into my thoughts. I blinked my eyes a few times to transfer myself back to reality. I froze, not knowing what to say to her.

"You haven't crossed out your last day yet. Here, let me help." She happily popped off the cap of the marker pen and put a big cross on the date of my calendar. "Now, your journey is complete." She winked at me as she put the cap back on.

Looking at the date with a black cross on it, I was amazed at how time had flown. When I gave my notice of resignation, I was supposed to serve for another two months to complete my employment contract. At that time, I immediately started my countdown by marking a cross on my calendar for each day I had left with the company. I started the countdown not because I was excited to leave the company but rather because I thought that I would dread the remaining two months. With each passing day, I thought that I would be treated as a coward who had walked away from a great challenge. I wanted my misery to end. I wanted to leave that place.

From the day I first entered the construction site until I tendered my resignation, a whole year had passed. The remaining two months, which initially seemed like a lifetime, also came to an end. Most of the experience that seemed excruciatingly painful to endure faded away with the passing of time.

I learnt many things during my employment at the company. Firstly, condition at the construction site was very harsh, but they toughened me up. In the end, I wasn't just a pale, skinny guy who read a lot and daydreamt when I was free. I still read a lot and daydreamt from time to time, but I also happened to be a kick-ass accountant at a construction site!

Secondly, I learnt the value of true friendship. I thought that making new friends at the workplace was impossible, but I stood corrected. Shan wasn't just a great boss; she was an understanding friend. She was there to share my joy when I was at my best, and she was there to support me when I was at my worst.

Every story had its endings. When a season ended, a new one began.

As I packed the last of my stuff into my box, I felt that I was ready to begin my new journey. I was a little sad about not having a huge impact on my friends and colleagues, but if I were to say that I had a tiny bit of influence, it was showing them that I had an undying passion towards my dream and I dared to give up everything in order to make it a reality.

Epilogue

What's Your Dream?

B ECOMING A JOBLESS ADULT WAS quite scary. I didn't have a safety net or a clear path waiting for me to travel. I hated the idea of updating my resume again. It had been a year since I had taken a good look at it. I also hated the long interview sessions that were conducted in small rooms. I couldn't go through those painful sessions again. I refused to fall back into the routine of working at a job I might potentially dislike.

Instead, I spent my time reading through my manuscript for the fourth time, going through every chapter, every paragraph, and every sentence. I was ready, or so I thought. I was glad that I had finally written a book, and yet I was afraid that the publisher wouldn't appreciate my efforts. I was afraid that readers wouldn't like my story. My thoughts were in a state of disarray.

Although there were mixed emotions in my head, overall, I was happy. I could finally recite the words that I told myself over the years, "You did it. You made your dream come true."

Technically, my book wasn't published yet at that point in time, but I didn't care. I was happy enough to have written one.

Dear readers, this is me, chasing my dream. I met a lot of people and encountered many speed bumps. Finally, here I am. It is important to have a dream. It doesn't matter whether it is big or small, as long as you have one. It keeps you alive. It makes you *want* to be alive.

If you feel that you don't have one now, take a break, travel, or just be alone and think about what you truly want in your life. Everyone wants different things in their lives, and everyone deserves a chance to chase their dreams.

What's your dream? It is time for you to chase it.

Printed in the United States
By Bookmasters